To Kids (and Parents)!

HEY KIDS! ARE YOU UP TO A TOOLBOX CHALLENGE?

If so, pick up a hard hat and grab a tool belt. There's a place for you on the G. H. Construction Crew. Can you guess what the G. H. stands for? (God's House) You say you don't know which end of a hammer to hold? Don't worry. We'll supply all the on-the-job training you'll need. As an Apprentice Crew Member (worker in training), you'll work daily at digging into the Bible and nailing down important truths. You'll also learn how to power up with prayer. Then you'll understand more of what it means to be a part of God's family, the church.

YOU'LL LEARN AND PRACTICE NEW SKILLS!

During the 50-day Adventure, you and thousands of other people will tackle the job of making God's House (the church) a better place. As a part of the crew, you'll learn about eight On-the-Job Training Topics and be asked to practice five important Crew Skills. These will help you to become one of Jesus' Journeymen (skilled workers). Want to know more? Then turn the page!

CHECK IT OUT

Before you join anything, it's always good to check it out first. The following information will tell you a few things you should know about G. H. Construction.

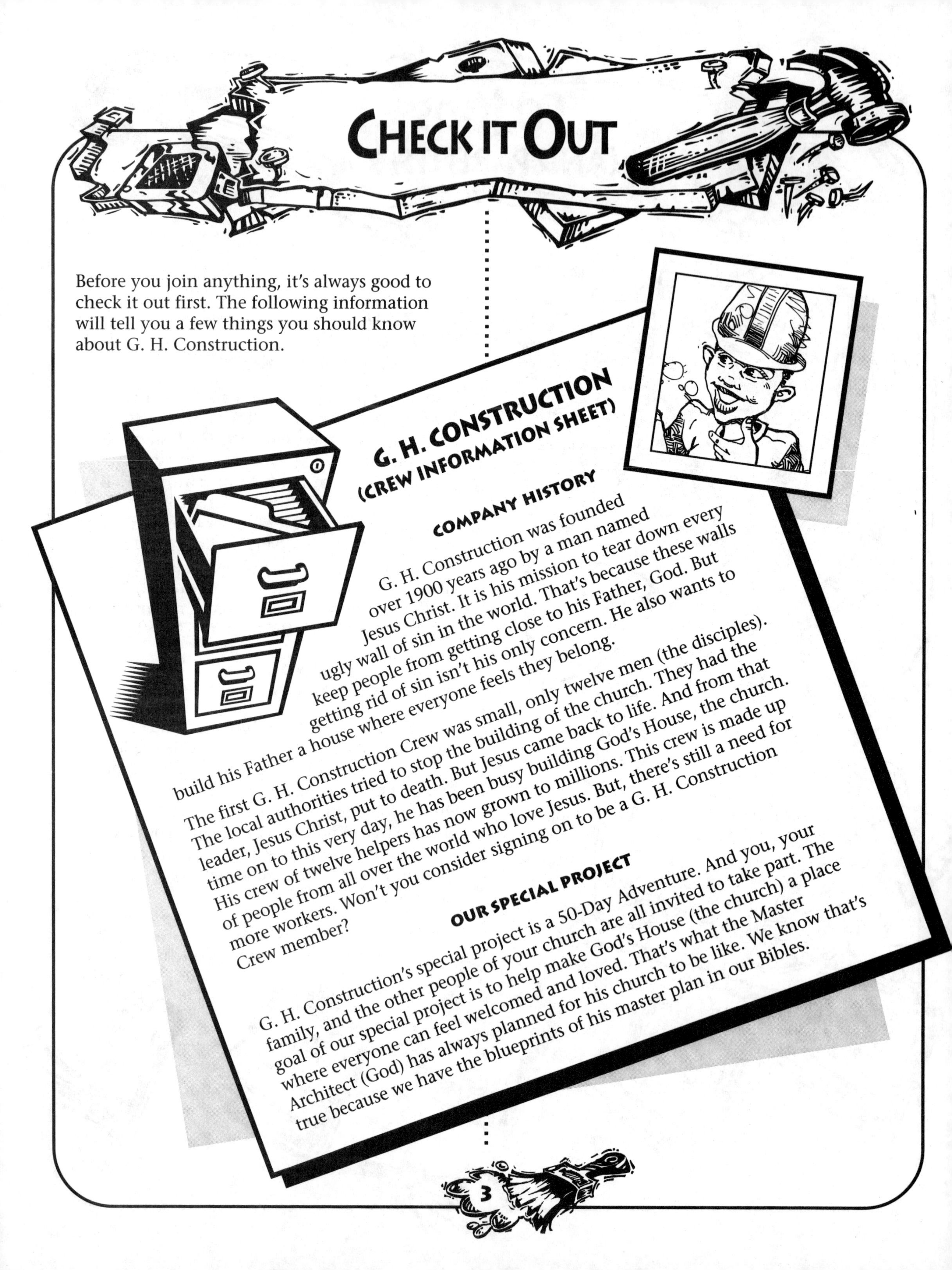

G. H. CONSTRUCTION (CREW INFORMATION SHEET)

COMPANY HISTORY

G. H. Construction was founded over 1900 years ago by a man named Jesus Christ. It is his mission to tear down every ugly wall of sin in the world. That's because these walls keep people from getting close to his Father, God. But getting rid of sin isn't his only concern. He also wants to build his Father a house where everyone feels they belong.

The first G. H. Construction Crew was small, only twelve men (the disciples). The local authorities tried to stop the building of the church. They had the leader, Jesus Christ, put to death. But Jesus came back to life. And from that time on to this very day, he has been busy building God's House, the church. His crew of twelve helpers has now grown to millions. This crew is made up of people from all over the world who love Jesus. But, there's still a need for more workers. Won't you consider signing on to be a G. H. Construction Crew member?

OUR SPECIAL PROJECT

G. H. Construction's special project is a 50-Day Adventure. And you, your family, and the other people of your church are all invited to take part. The goal of our special project is to help make God's House (the church) a place where everyone can feel welcomed and loved. That's what the Master Architect (God) has always planned for his church to be like. We know that's true because we have the blueprints of his master plan in our Bibles.

ORGANIZE YOUR TOOLS

Before reporting to work as an apprentice, you will need to gather the following tools:

1. YOUR BIBLE. It's important that every crew member check out God's master plan each day. To do this, you will need a Bible. It doesn't matter which kind of Bible you have as long as it is easy for you to read and understand. Your daily work assignment will include a Scripture passage to read and think about. You will also have a Bible Blueprint (memory verse) to learn each week.

2. YOUR JOURNAL. This journal is your apprentice handbook. It gives you all the information you need to do your job. As you look through it, you will notice that there is an activity for each day of the Adventure. Plan to report to work every day.

If you're the kind of kid who likes to set goals, make sure you read "How to Become a Journeyman" on page 11. It could add some extra fun and challenge to the Adventure. If becoming a journeyman doesn't interest you, that's OK.

3. A GOOD ATTITUDE. Our Crew Foreman (Jesus Christ) wants happy workers. So you will find a bit of fun tucked here and there throughout the journal.

4. A GOOD POWER SOURCE. In order to get things done right, we need a dependable power source to plug into. God is our power source on this project. So plan to use the Power Source Prayer on page 1 every day. With God's help, you can play a real part in making your church or church club not just good, but great! It can become a place where everyone feels they belong.

HOW TO USE YOUR JOURNAL

WHAT DOES A G. H. CONSTRUCTION CREW APPRENTICE ACTUALLY DO?

You've probably already flipped through the pages of this journal to see what it's like. And so you've noticed that there is one journal activity page for each day of the Adventure. Each activity page has the following four work projects on it.

▶ 1. CHECK THE MASTER PLAN

This includes looking up and reading a Bible passage. The Bible Blueprint Verse will be introduced each Saturday. You will be reminded to practice it in the Crew Skill Practice section mentioned below.

▶ 2. THINK ABOUT IT

This is some extra information to help you understand the Bible passage.

▶ 3. THE CARPENTER'S PENCIL

This is a puzzle, maze, code, or some other kind of pencil activity.

▶ 4. CREW SKILL PRACTICE

This is a short list of ideas on how to put the five Crew Skills to use. (Remember the Crew Skills mentioned on page 2? They're an important part of your Adventure.) And every Saturday there's a "Level Check" to help you keep track of your Crew Skills.

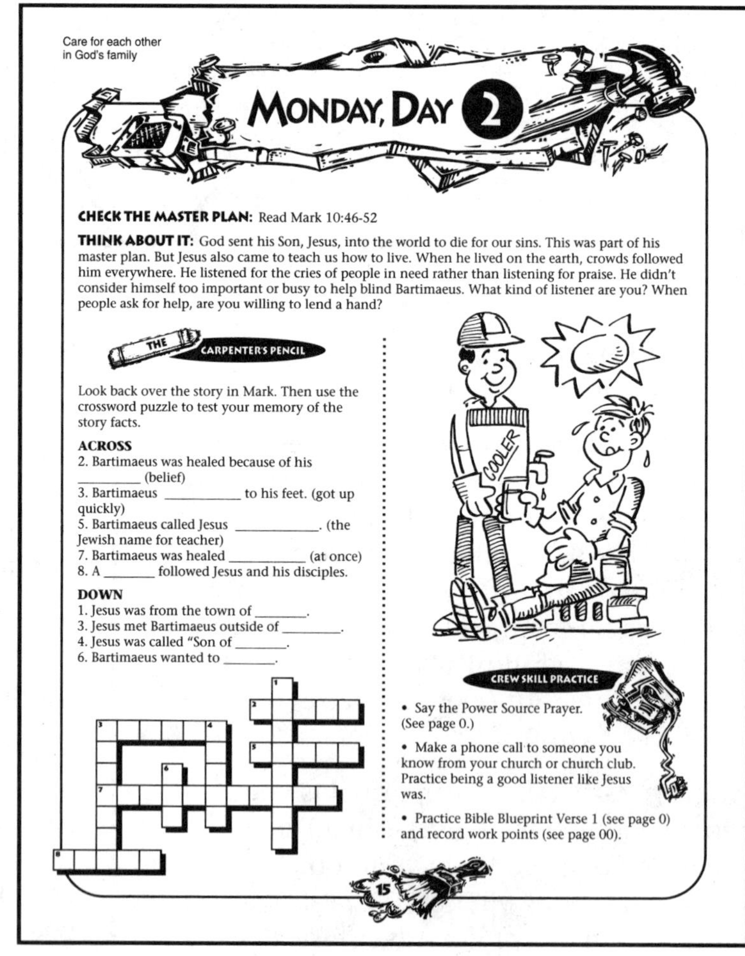

Care for each other in God's family

MONDAY, DAY 2

CHECK THE MASTER PLAN: Read Mark 10:46-52

THINK ABOUT IT: God sent his Son, Jesus, into the world to die for our sins. This was part of his master plan. But Jesus also came to teach us how to live. When he lived on the earth, crowds followed him everywhere. He listened for the cries of people in need rather than listening for praise. He didn't consider himself too important or busy to help blind Bartimaeus. What kind of listener are you? When people ask for help, are you willing to lend a hand?

THE CARPENTER'S PENCIL

Look back over the story in Mark. Then use the crossword puzzle to test your memory of the story facts.

ACROSS
2. Bartimaeus was healed because of his ________ (belief)
3. Bartimaeus __________ to his feet. (got up quickly)
5. Bartimaeus called Jesus ___________. (the Jewish name for teacher)
7. Bartimaeus was healed __________ (at once)
8. A _______ followed Jesus and his disciples.

DOWN
1. Jesus was from the town of ________.
3. Jesus met Bartimaeus outside of _________.
4. Jesus was called "Son of _______.
6. Bartimaeus wanted to ________.

CREW SKILL PRACTICE

- Say the Power Source Prayer. (See page 0.)
- Make a phone call to someone you know from your church or church club. Practice being a good listener like Jesus was.
- Practice Bible Blueprint Verse 1 (see page 0) and record work points (see page 00).

15

Setting Your Schedule

HOW MUCH TIME SHOULD IT TAKE?

It should take between 10 and 15 minutes to complete a journal page. (Give or take a few minutes for speed reading or dawdling.)

If you're like most kids your age, your days can be pretty busy. When you don't have enough time to do all of a day's activities, try to do at least the Crew Skill Practice. If you happen to miss a day or two completely, skip those pages and go on. It takes at least three weeks to get a new habit started. So if you aren't already in the habit of setting aside time each day to read the Bible and pray, you'll have to work at it.

Think about your daily routine. What seems like the best time for you to work in your journal? If you aren't sure, talk with your mom or dad about it. Whatever time of day you choose, try to work in your journal the same time each day. This will help you remember to do it. Draw the numbers and hands on the watch to show the time you've chosen.

FIND A GOOD PLACE TO WORK.

Another helpful tip is to find a comfortable, quiet place to work. Then keep your journal, pencil, and Bible there. If it's not practical to leave your things unattended because of pets or little brothers or sisters, put your supplies in a box and put the box in a safe place. You might want to make the box look like a toolbox. Print the following on the side: Property of G. H. Construction, Apprentice (your name).

MASTER THE 5 CREW SKILLS

We've identified five skills that apprentices need to learn. They're skills you can put to use everywhere—church, home, school, club, or sport team. The following information will explain what you will be asked to do in the Crew Skill Practice section of each daily page.

CREW SKILL 1:

LISTEN TO OTHERS THE WAY JESUS WOULD.

Have you ever tried to talk to someone and had a hard time getting the person to listen? Well, Jesus isn't like that. He really listens. He wants to know what people are thinking and feeling so he can help them. Everyone he met on earth knew that he really cared about them because of the way he listened. As an apprentice, you will be challenged to follow the example of our Crew Foreman (Jesus) and become a better listener. It won't always be easy, but God will help you if you ask him.

There are two ways to practice Crew Skill 1.

Plug into God's power source each day using the Power Source Prayer on page 1.

Make it a point to ask people how things are going for them. If they tell you about a problem, promise to pray for them. And then do it.

You will learn more about this skill during Week 1 of the Adventure. The journal will remind you to practice this Crew Skill every day.

Master the 5 Crew Skills

Crew Skill 2:

Say good things about your church.

Have you ever wanted to see a movie that all your friends said they hated? Probably not. Would you buy an outfit that your best friend laughed at? Probably not. Whether they're right or wrong, most of our opinions are influenced by what others say. When we criticize things, we can make other people dislike them. And when we praise things, we can make people interested in them. One way you can help the church or your church club grow bigger is by letting others know what's good about it. Just because your church or club might not be perfect, that doesn't mean there aren't plenty of good things to say.

There are three ways to practice this skill:

1. For fun, try to think of 50 good things to say about your church and the people in your church. (If you go to a church club, you may want to write about it.) Write your list of compliments on pages 33–34.

2. At least once a week, tell a friend something nice about your church or church club.

3. Sometime during this Adventure invite a friend to come to church or church club.

You'll find out more about this skill in Week 2 of the Adventure.

Crew Skill 3:

Be caring and make a new friend.

Have you ever moved or changed schools? If you have, then you know it can be hard to make new friends. But you've also had the chance to learn that a little friendliness on your part can be the start of a new friendship. Church should be a place where everyone feels welcome. But just because it should be a friendly place, that doesn't mean it always is.

Do you look for your friends as soon as you get to church or your church club, and then talk only to them? Do you ever invite kids you don't know very well to join you and your friends? Or do you just walk by them week after week as if they were invisible? How do you decide who you want as a friend? Are you only interested in kids who are like you? Or are you willing to be friendly to people who are different from you?

Master the 5 Crew Skills

There are two ways to practice Crew Skill 3.

Smile and say hello to someone new at church, church club, or school.

Try to make one new friend before the Adventure is over. This can be someone in your neighborhood, school, club, sports team, or at church.

You will find out more about this skill during Week 3.

Crew Skill 4:

Put your talents to use.

Have you ever noticed how many different kinds of insects or flowers there are? God likes variety! He didn't just make a flower, he made lots of flowers. And he didn't just make an insect, he made thousands of insects! They come in all sizes, shapes, and colors. Some hop, some dig, some fly, and some do all three plus walk on water.

God made people different, too. We're good at lots of different things. Have you discovered some of the things you do really well? Our differences make the world a more beautiful and interesting place. As a G. H. Construction Crew Apprentice, you will be challenged to find out what special talents you have. And you might even help other people discover theirs. Church should be a place where everyone can feel appreciated and needed, a place where everyone gets to shine from time to time. How are you using your talents to serve God?

There are three ways to practice Crew Skill 4.

1. Get to know yourself better. Keep a list of the things you do well.
2. Volunteer to do something that uses your talents. This can be done at church, school, home, club, wherever.
3. Compliment someone for something you think he or she does well.

You'll find out more about this skill during Week 4.

MASTER THE 5 CREW SKILLS

CREW SKILL 5:

CLEAN UP GARBAGE THOUGHTS AND ACTIONS.

Most churches are neat and clean before everyone arrives. But when the church doors open and people come in, dirt and disorder come in too. It takes a lot of work to keep a church building clean. But a church building isn't the only thing God's people need to keep clean. We need to keep our hearts and minds clean too. The things we love and spend our time thinking about affect what we say and do. And the things we say and do affect the way people feel about God's church. What do your words and actions tell people about God's family? Would they want to be a part of God's family because of the kind of person you are?

There are three ways to practice Crew Skill 5.

Take a good look at what you choose to do for fun. Does it make you more like Jesus or less like him?

Listen to yourself carefully. Do your words sound like something Jesus would say?

3 Make a list of things that are garbage thoughts and actions. You will be shown how to do this on Day 28 of the Adventure. You need to clean up your room on a regular basis. You also need to clean out the garbage thoughts and actions from your life on a regular basis.

You'll find out more about this skill during Week 5.

BIBLE BLUEPRINT MEMORY VERSES

1. Dear friends, since God so loved us, we also ought to love one another. 1 John 4:11 (NIV)

▶ **2.** I will praise you, O Lord, with all my heart; I will tell of all your wonders. Psalm 9:1 (NIV)

▶ **3.** God accepts anyone who worships him and does what is right. It is not important what country a person comes from. Acts 10:35 (ICB)

▶ **4.** Each one should use whatever gift he has received to serve others. 1 Peter 4:10a (NIV)

▶ **5.** Be a worker who is not ashamed of his work—a worker who uses the true teaching in the right way. 2 Timothy 2:15b (ICB)

▶ **6.** You should feed those who are hungry. You should take care of the needs of those who are troubled. Isaiah 58:10a (ICB)

▶ **7.** It is good to praise the Lord, to sing praises to God Most High. Psalm 92:1 (ICB)

▶ **8.** You are a chosen people, . . . a people belonging to God, that you may declare the praises of him who called you out of darkness into his wonderful light. 1 Peter 2:9 (NIV)

How to Become a Journeyman

(Optional Activity)

If you like the challenge of working toward a goal, then here's a fun idea for you to try. Work your way up from being an apprentice (worker in training) to becoming a journeyman (skilled worker). You do this by earning points for the daily journal activities you complete. A score of 800 points is a good goal to shoot for.

HERE IS HOW TO SCORE YOUR WORK:

Check the Master Plan—5 points

Think About It—5 points

The Carpenter's Pencil—5 points

Crew Skill Practice (all skills listed each day)—10 points

Miscellaneous—(bonus points as listed on pages throughout the journal)

Keep track of your points on a separate piece of paper. Or record them on the bottom of each journal page. At the end of the Adventure add up your points. Then decorate the picture on this page. Cut along the dotted line and use it as a bookmark for your Bible. You may also want to have a celebration with your family or friends. Doing the Adventure represents a lot of hard work. Congratulations!

Warm-up Friday

Inspection Day

Have you ever watched a TV home improvement program? What happens first before any construction work is started? That's right. The building is inspected to see what needs to be fixed. One of the first things checked is the foundation. If the foundation isn't good, the building is in big trouble. It might even fall down!

Let's inspect the foundation of God's House (the church).

LOOK UP
1 CORINTHIANS 3:9–11
(and answer questions 1–2 at right).

CREW SKILL PRACTICE

- Plug into God's power by using the Power Source Prayer on page 1 of this journal. Ask God to help you become more caring for others.
- Record your work points. (See page 11.)

1. What or who is the foundation? (Verse 11)

2. How old is the foundation? (You might need to ask for help with this one.)

NOW READ EPHESIANS 2:19–22.

3. What does God want built on this foundation? (Verses 19–22)

4. Take a good look at the foundation below. Can you read what is written on it?

ANSWERS: 1. JESUS CHRIST 2. MORE THAN 1900 YEARS OLD 3. HIS HOLY TEMPLE (THE CHURCH) 4. JESUS

Warm-Up Saturday

For the next few weeks you and the other crew members will be tackling the job of helping to improve your church in these eight areas. The journal will help you understand what you can do. The first thing you can do is to care for others in God's family. That's what our Bible Blueprint Verse is all about.

INSPECTION DAY

Look over the eight phrases that describe a strong church. Circle **G** if your church is in great shape, **O** if it is OK, **D** if it could do better or if you don't know the answer.

1. Acts like a caring family **G O D**
2. Has a good reputation **G O D**
3. Welcomes everyone **G O D**
4. Gives everyone a chance to put their talents to use **G O D**
5. Works at keeping garbage thoughts, words, and actions cleaned up **G O D**
6. Cares about people around the world **G O D**
7. Is a good place to get to know God better **G O D**
8. Gives people a reason to be happy about the future **G O D**

VERSE 1—BIBLE BLUEPRINT VERSE CHECK

The verse for Week 1 is 1 John 4:11. Unscramble the words of the verse, then write them in order on the stacked bricks. (Turn to page 10 to check your work.)

God one friends, to another.
Dear also us, since loved we
ought so love

CREW SKILL PRACTICE

- Remember to power up with the Power Source Prayer on page 1.
- Start memorizing this week's Bible Blueprint Verse. (See page 10 for help.)
- Record your work points. (See page 11.)

On-the-Job Training Topic for Week 1:
Care for each other
in God's family

SUNDAY, DAY 1

CHECK THE MASTER PLAN:
Read Acts 2:42–47

THINK ABOUT IT: The first Christians sound like interesting people, don't they? They were really excited about what they believed, and it changed their lives. These events took place soon after the Jewish feast of Pentecost (a holiday similar to Thanksgiving). People from all over the world came to Jerusalem to bring their offerings to God's temple. Jerusalem was one crowded city! What a perfect time for God to send his Holy Spirit to power up the twelve apostles and Jesus' other followers. Now they were ready to go out and invite others to God's church. In fact, on one day when the apostle Peter preached, 3,000 people believed in Jesus!

THE CARPENTER'S PENCIL

Answer these questions based on what you read in Acts.

1. These first believers felt awe for God. Have you ever felt this way about something you've seen God do? What? ______________________

____

2. Did their attitudes about the things they owned change when they became believers? ______________ How? ______________________

____

3. What did they enjoy doing together? ______

____

4. What did other people think about them?

____

____

____

CREW SKILL PRACTICE

- Look around at church and school for people who may need prayer. Pray for one of them in your Power Source Prayers (page 1) this week.
- Practice this week's Bible Blueprint Memory Verse. (See page 10 for help.)
- Record your work points. (See page 11.)

CHECK THE MASTER PLAN: Read Mark 10:46–52

THINK ABOUT IT: God sent his Son, Jesus, into the world to die for our sins. This was part of his master plan. But Jesus also came to teach us how to live. When he lived on the earth, crowds followed him everywhere. He listened for the cries of people in need rather than listening for praise. He didn't consider himself too important or busy to help blind Bartimaeus. What kind of listener are you? When people ask for help, are you willing to lend a hand?

Look back over the story in Mark. Then use the crossword puzzle to test your memory of the story facts.

ACROSS

2. Bartimaeus was healed because of his _________. (belief)
3. Bartimaeus __________ to his feet. (got up quickly)
5. Bartimaeus called Jesus ___________. (the Jewish name for teacher)
7. Bartimaeus was healed ___________. (at once)
8. A ________ followed Jesus and his disciples.

DOWN

1. Jesus was from the town of _______.
3. Jesus met Bartimaeus outside of ________.
4. Jesus was called "Son of _______."
6. Bartimaeus wanted to _______.

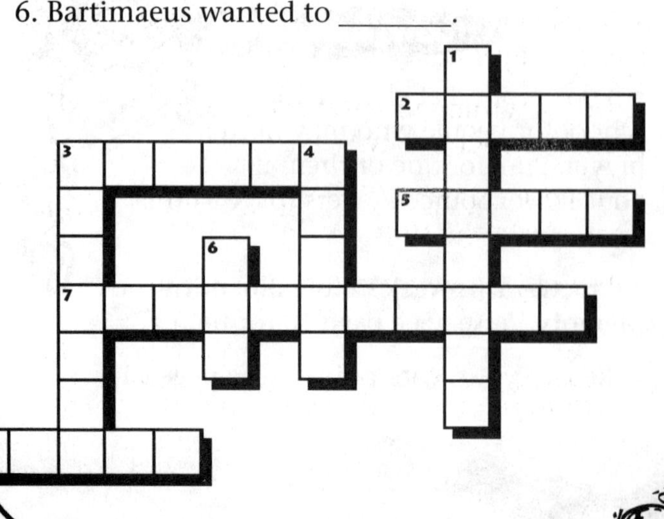

CREW SKILL PRACTICE

- Say the Power Source Prayer. (See page 1.)
- Make a phone call to someone you know from your church or church club. Practice being a good listener like Jesus was.
- Practice Bible Blueprint Verse 1 (see page 10) and record work points (see page 11).

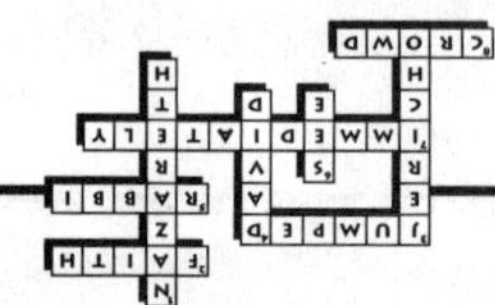

Care for each other in God's family

TUESDAY, DAY 3

CHECK THE MASTER PLAN: Read Romans 12:9–16

Love	**Good**
Hate	**Evil**
Cling to	**From your heart**
-------	-------
Honor	**Proud**
Serve	**Peace**
Live in	**Others**
Be not	**The Lord**

THINK ABOUT IT: In these verses Paul explains how Christians should love each other. Love isn't just a good feeling, it's an action. When we truly love other people, we show it by what we do for them. When people love one another, they give each other support (hold each other up) in good times and bad. Love, like a strong support beam, is what holds friendships together. How strong are your friendships?

THE CARPENTER'S PENCIL

Connect the two beams by drawing lines to match the words on the left with the words on the right. If you do these things you will help your friendships to grow strong. (Hint: There may be more than one right answer for some.)

CREW SKILL PRACTICE

- Remember to use the Power Source Prayer today. (See page 1.)
- Do something nice today for each person in your family.
- Practice this week's Bible Blueprint Verse. (See page 10.)
- Record your work points. (See page 11.)

ANSWERS: LOVE—FROM YOUR HEART, HATE—EVIL, CLING TO—GOOD, HONOR—OTHERS, SERVE—THE LORD, LIVE IN—PEACE, BE NOT—PROUD

CHECK THE MASTER PLAN:
Read 1 John 4:7–12

THINK ABOUT IT: The common cold is contagious. That's why the crew member on the right looks a bit worried. No one wants to catch a cold. All that sneezing, coughing, stuffiness, and body aching . . . Ugh! If you've caught a cold bug, you look and act like you have one. But just because something is contagious, that doesn't make it bad. The verses you just read in 1 John tell us that God's love is contagious. Everyone who knows God well will be filled with his love. And this love will show in the things we say and do. Are you showing God's love to people?

1. How did God prove his love to us?__________

____

2. Draw a picture of the most loving person you know.

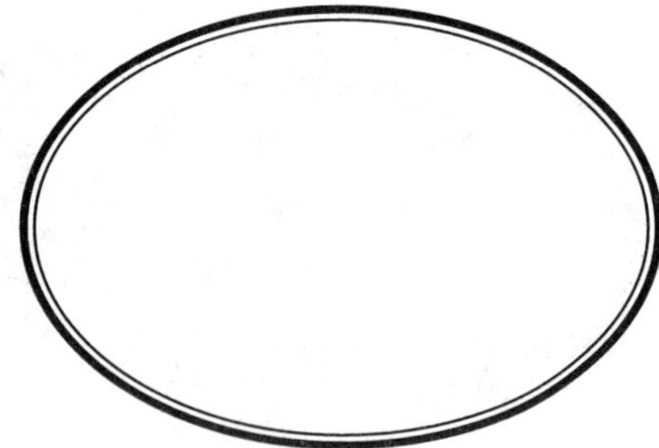

Name: ______________________________

3. Where did he or she learn to be so caring? (If you don't know, ask the person.)

____

CREW SKILL PRACTICE

- Don't forget to use the Power Source Prayer today. (See page 1.) Ask God to help you learn to be more loving.
- Smile at at least five people. (One could be someone you don't know.)
- Practice Bible Blueprint Verse 1. (See page 10 for help.)
- Record your work points. (See page 11.)

(5 Bonus Points)

Make stone "Love Bugs" to give to your friends and family members. Gather and wash several small rocks. Then paint them red and black to look like lady bugs. (Acrylic paint works well.) Make the spots on the bugs' backs heart-shaped. Give the bugs away with notes that say "Since God so loved us, we also ought to love one another." (1 John 4:11)

THURSDAY, DAY 5

CHECK THE MASTER PLAN: Read 2 Samuel 9:1–13

THINK ABOUT IT: Life was finally turning out good for King David. He no longer had to run away from King Saul or fight Saul's family for the throne. His army captured the city of Jerusalem, and he made it his capital city. He got married and had several sons and daughters. And he lived in a palace. But instead of just enjoying the good life, he looked for someone he could help. That's what God wants us to do with the blessings he gives us. He wants us to care for each other.

THE CARPENTER'S PENCIL

Here are the names of the six men in our Bible story today. Find the names in the word search puzzle. Remember, the names can be located diagonally, forward, or backward. Draw a heart around the name of the most helpful person.

DAVID ZIBA SAUL

JONATHAN MAKIR MEPHIBOSHETH

```
R I N A H T A N O J K H
I L Z I B E L S Z D T T
K O U S N O J A U E Z J
O M K A B O S U H V O S
J A P U S R K S I E T B
O K H I D T O Z Y E H L
N I I D I B R Z D R Z S
D R B V I C T I A T H H
R T O H I K V B K Z P H
A K P V A A K A A I E E
K E B E D O I R U B T T
M R N V Z U A S I L H H
```

CREW SKILL PRACTICE

- Power up God's love by using the Power Source Prayer today. (See page 1.)
- Ask two people if there is something you can do to help them.
- Keep working on Bible Blueprint Verse 1. (See page 10 for help.)
- Don't forget to record your work points. (See page 11.)

Has anyone ever given you or your family a helping hand? What did they do?

____

____

ANSWERS:

FRIDAY, DAY 6

CHECK THE MASTER PLAN:
Read Philippians 2:1–4

THINK ABOUT IT: "What's in it for me?" "How can I go first?" "How can I get the biggest piece or best part?" "How can I get things done my way?" Have you ever asked yourself questions like these? Maybe you didn't use these exact words, but you found yourself looking out for "Number 1"— YOU! Well, you're not alone. Selfishness seems to be natural for humans. But that's not how God wants us to be. God wants us to have the same

(GOTTHHUS) ______________________

as Jesus and his unselfish **(VOEL)** __________ for everyone. He wants his church to be the kind of loving family everyone would like to be a part of. (Unscramble the 2 words above.)

The world God holds in his hands is a troubled world, isn't it? Use the lines to list two problems in your life. Then circle "yes" if selfishness helped cause the problems and "no" if it didn't.

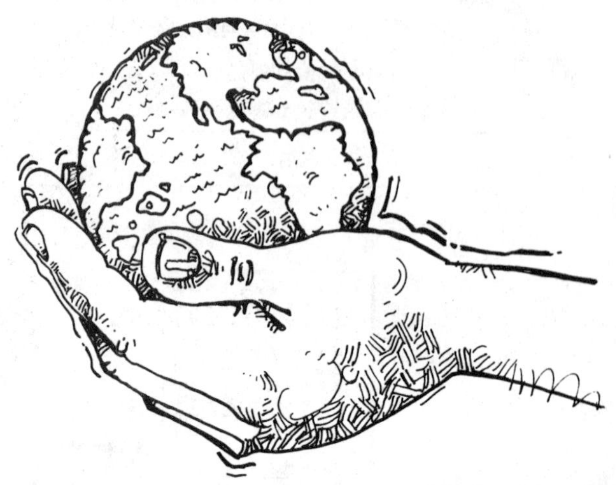

(For example: Your problem might be saying mean things about your next-door neighbors. The reason is that they have something you think you should have. This is a kind of selfishness.)

1. ______________________ **YES NO**
2. ______________________ **YES NO**

CREW SKILL PRACTICE

- As you power up with prayer today, ask God to help you with the problems you wrote about. (See page 1.)
- Last day to learn Bible Blueprint Verse 1. (See page 10 for help.) Don't give up!
- Record your work points. (See page 11.)

(5 Bonus Points)

Take a look at today's newspaper or listen to a news broadcast. For each problem mentioned, try to figure out if selfishness created the problem. (For example, if someone was stealing money, maybe it was because he or she wanted to be rich.) Who was being selfish? And how would the situation have changed if everyone followed Philippians 2:1–4? (This would be a good subject to talk about with your family or friends.)

On-the-Job Training Topic for Week 2:
Get the word out to
your friends

SATURDAY, DAY 7

LEVEL CHECK

WEEK 2 (5 POINTS)

This is the start of Week 2 of the Adventure. How did you do last week? Were you able to find time most days to work in your journal? Well, if not, don't worry. You can start fresh today. This week you'll learn how to help your church or club grow by telling people good things about it. You'll find it helpful to review Crew Skill 2 on page 8.

BIBLE BLUEPRINT

VERSE CHECK

VERSE 2 (5 POINTS)

Turn to page 10 to find this week's verse. It is from the Book of Psalms. Psalms are ancient worship songs. King David wrote many of the psalms with God's help. We don't know the tunes anymore, but the words still tell us important truths. This verse is about telling others the great things God does for us.

THE CARPENTER'S PENCIL

Here's a fun idea to help you practice this week's Bible Blueprint Verse. Fan-fold a sheet of

notebook paper. Then open it up. Write the words of the verse on the paper as shown.

To use the fan-folded paper to practice the verse, view it on an angle. First, hold it so that the left side is closest to you. Read the words that you can see and try saying from memory the words you can't see. Then hold the paper with the right side closest to you and do the same thing.

CREW SKILL PRACTICE

- Plug into the Power Source Prayer. Choose someone new to pray for this week.
- Start your list of 50 good things you can say about your church or church club. (See pages 33–34.)
- Record your work points. (See page 11.)

SUNDAY, DAY 8

CHECK THE MASTER PLAN:
Read Acts 5:12–16

THINK ABOUT IT: Talk about good news traveling fast! These people didn't even have phones or TV. Imagine what you would do if you learned that someone you knew had discovered the cure for AIDS or cancer. Would you spread the word? Peter must have been thrilled to be given God's power to heal people. But he knew that he had something more important to do than healing. He had good news to tell. The good news is that we can be forgiven for our sins because of Jesus.

CREW SKILL PRACTICE

• Power up with the Power Source Prayer. The next time you see the person you're praying for, be sure to smile and say hello.

• Add two more church compliments to your list. (See Crew Skill 2, page 8.)

• Tell someone you know about something good that happened at church.

• Work on Bible Blueprint Verse 2 (page 10) and record your work points.

OVERTIME OPPORTUNITY

(10 Bonus Points)

Write your teacher a note. Tell him or her something you like about your class.

THE CARPENTER'S PENCIL

Create an ad about your church or church club for the local paper or radio station. What will you say? A good ad lets people know that you have something they need. And it says it in a fun or interesting way. Do your creative work in the space provided.

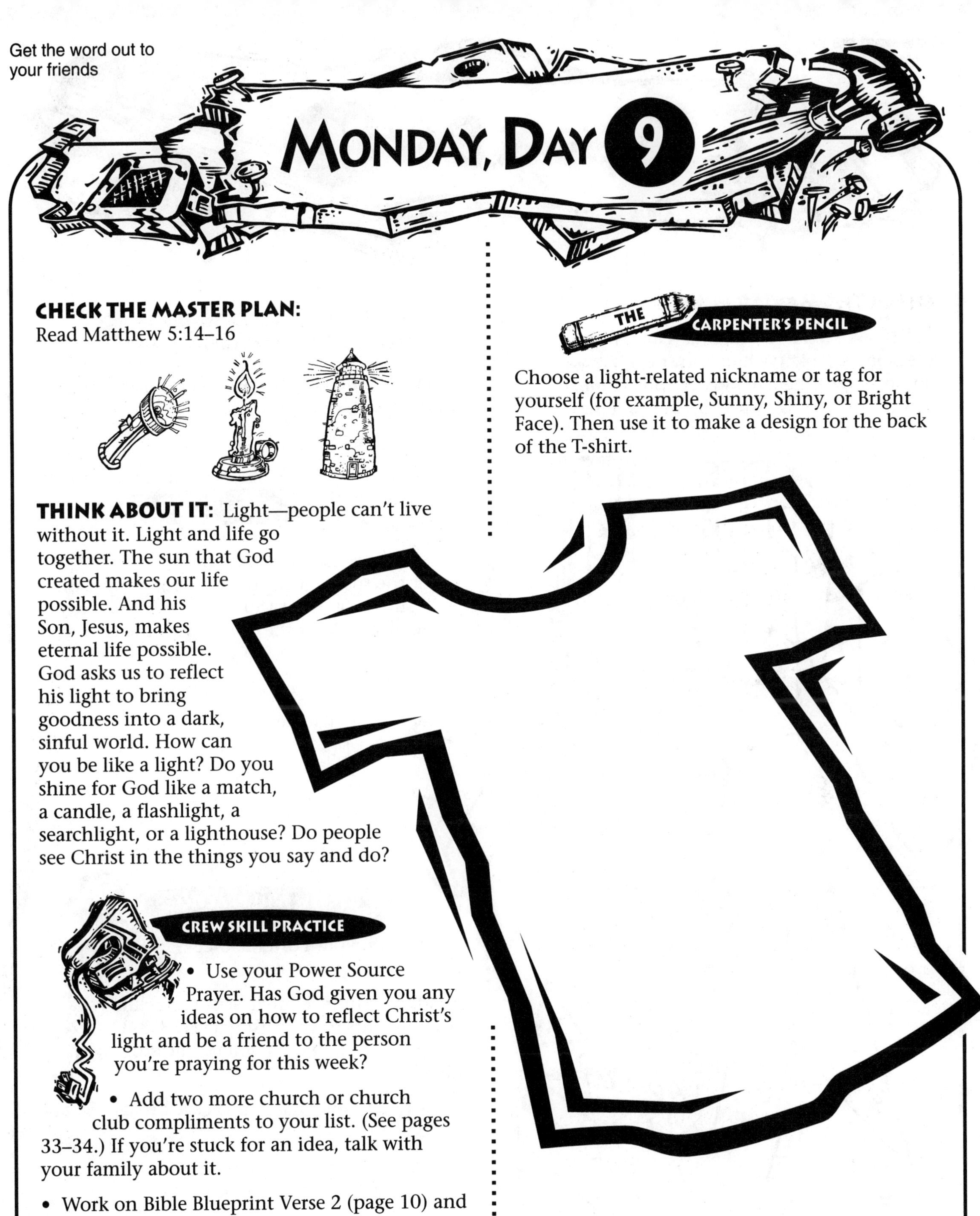

MONDAY, DAY 9

CHECK THE MASTER PLAN:
Read Matthew 5:14–16

THINK ABOUT IT: Light—people can't live without it. Light and life go together. The sun that God created makes our life possible. And his Son, Jesus, makes eternal life possible. God asks us to reflect his light to bring goodness into a dark, sinful world. How can you be like a light? Do you shine for God like a match, a candle, a flashlight, a searchlight, or a lighthouse? Do people see Christ in the things you say and do?

CREW SKILL PRACTICE

- Use your Power Source Prayer. Has God given you any ideas on how to reflect Christ's light and be a friend to the person you're praying for this week?
- Add two more church or church club compliments to your list. (See pages 33–34.) If you're stuck for an idea, talk with your family about it.
- Work on Bible Blueprint Verse 2 (page 10) and record your work points.

THE CARPENTER'S PENCIL

Choose a light-related nickname or tag for yourself (for example, Sunny, Shiny, or Bright Face). Then use it to make a design for the back of the T-shirt.

TUESDAY, DAY 10

CHECK THE MASTER PLAN: Read Acts 9:36–43

THINK ABOUT IT: Tabitha (Dorcas) seems to have been a very special person. She was loved by everyone who knew her. And she is the only woman called a "disciple" in the New Testament. That doesn't mean that she was the only woman to be a follower of Christ. What it means is that she earned everyone's respect because she served Christ by helping others.

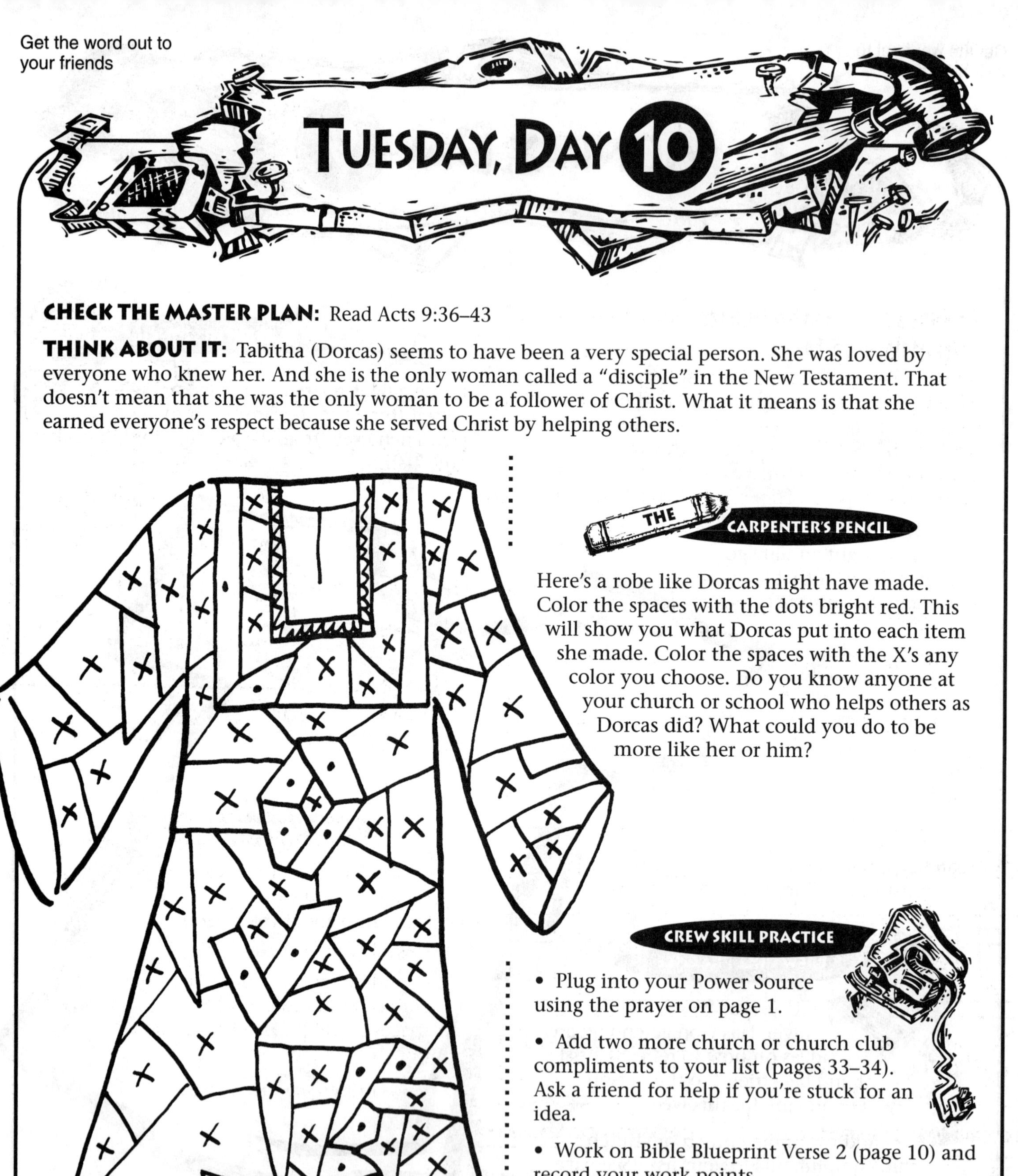

THE CARPENTER'S PENCIL

Here's a robe like Dorcas might have made. Color the spaces with the dots bright red. This will show you what Dorcas put into each item she made. Color the spaces with the X's any color you choose. Do you know anyone at your church or school who helps others as Dorcas did? What could you do to be more like her or him?

CREW SKILL PRACTICE

- Plug into your Power Source using the prayer on page 1.
- Add two more church or church club compliments to your list (pages 33–34). Ask a friend for help if you're stuck for an idea.
- Work on Bible Blueprint Verse 2 (page 10) and record your work points.

Get the word out to your friends

CHECK THE MASTER PLAN: Read Philippians 2:14–16

THINK ABOUT IT: It's a sore-thumb world. Everywhere you look people are hurting. The problems of life just keeping giving them a whack! There is divorce, sickness, and people fighting with each other. This is not the way God wants the world to be, but sin has made it this way. Jesus has asked his followers to take care of each other. By doing this, they can show the world a better way to live.

Use the first aid supplies to decode four things you can do to help others.

Who can you do one of those things for this week? ______________________

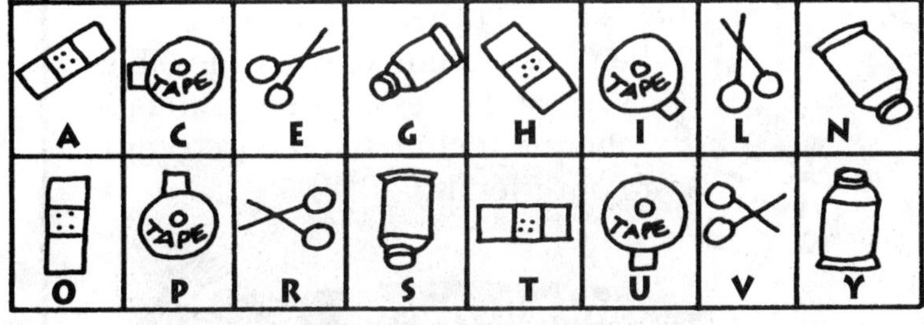

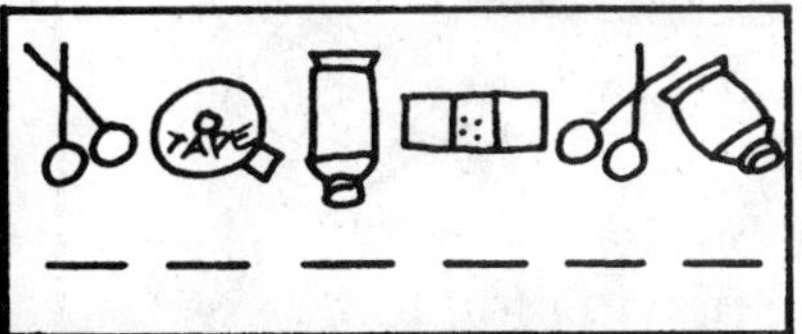

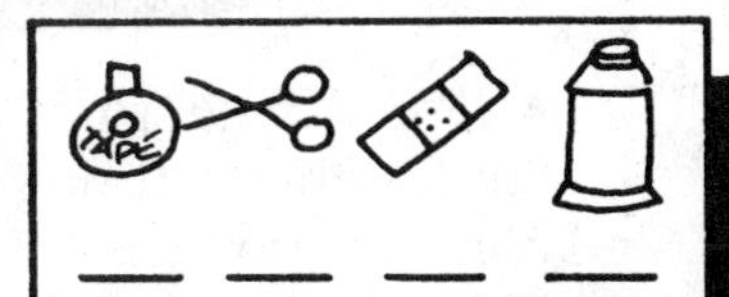

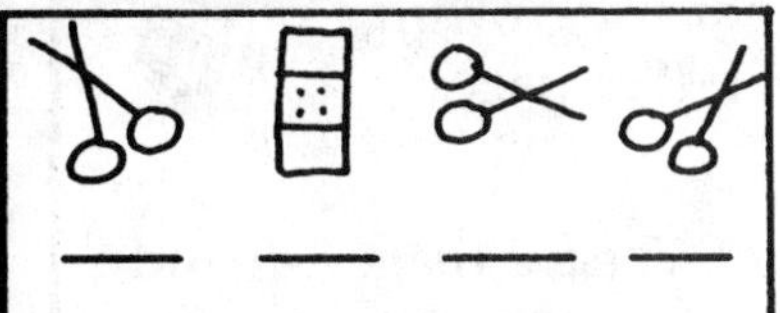

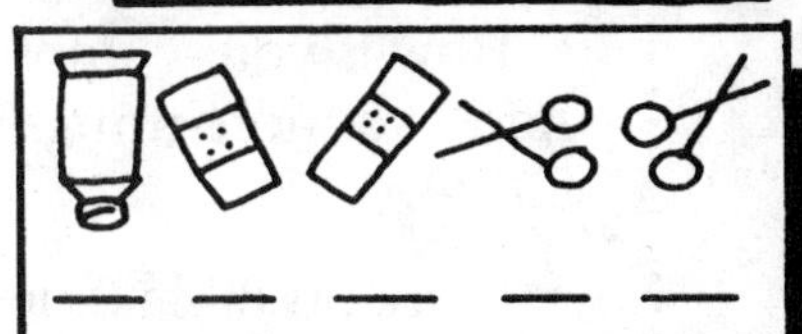

CREW SKILL PRACTICE

- Plug into your Power Source Prayer (page 1). Tell God something nice about the person you're praying for.
- Add two more church or church club compliments to your list (pages 33–34.). Tell a friend about one of them.
- Record your work points.

ANSWERS: LISTEN, PRAY, LOVE, SHARE

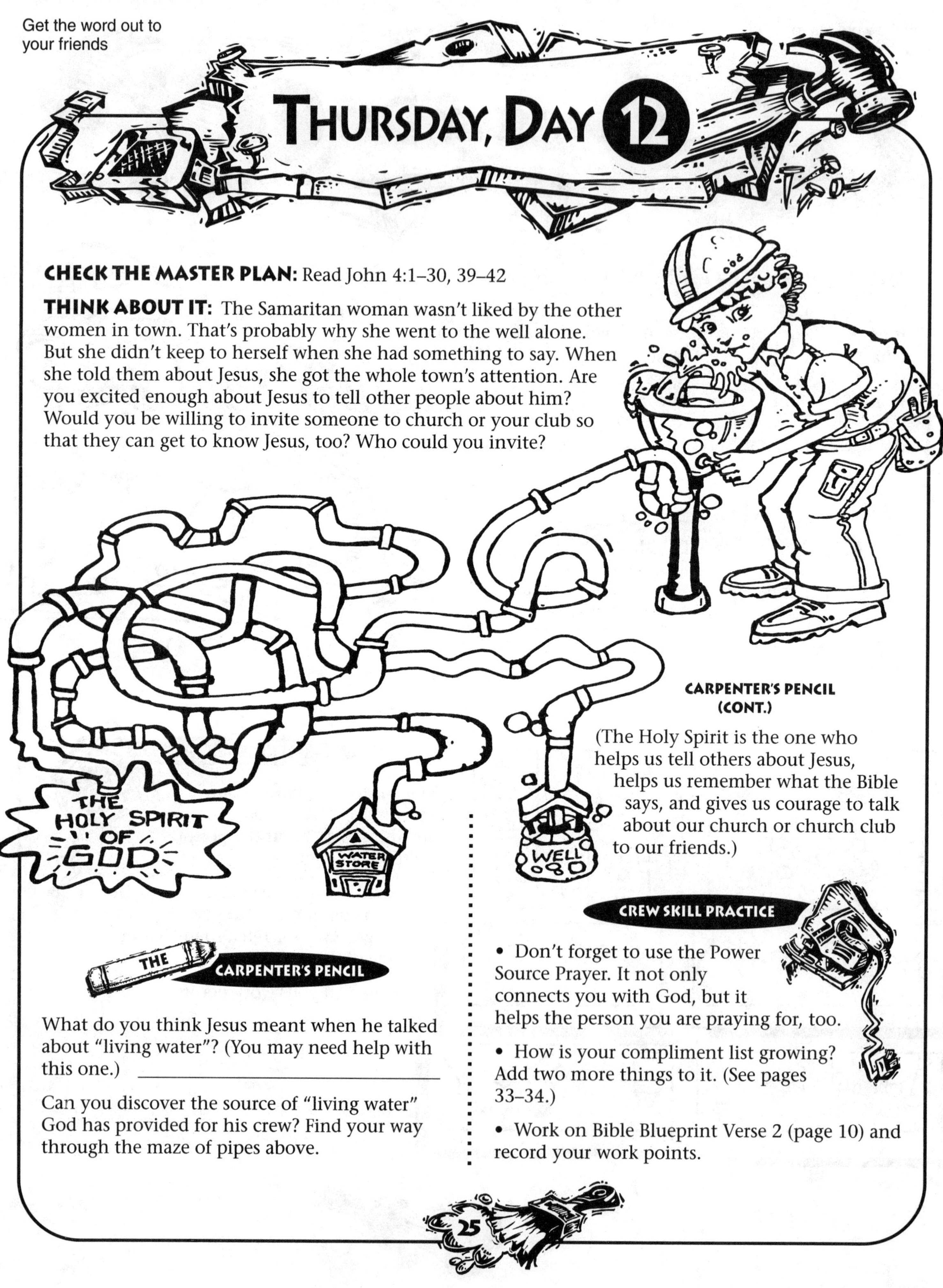

THURSDAY, DAY 12

CHECK THE MASTER PLAN: Read John 4:1–30, 39–42

THINK ABOUT IT: The Samaritan woman wasn't liked by the other women in town. That's probably why she went to the well alone. But she didn't keep to herself when she had something to say. When she told them about Jesus, she got the whole town's attention. Are you excited enough about Jesus to tell other people about him? Would you be willing to invite someone to church or your club so that they can get to know Jesus, too? Who could you invite?

THE CARPENTER'S PENCIL

What do you think Jesus meant when he talked about "living water"? (You may need help with this one.) ______________________________

Can you discover the source of "living water" God has provided for his crew? Find your way through the maze of pipes above.

CARPENTER'S PENCIL (CONT.)

(The Holy Spirit is the one who helps us tell others about Jesus, helps us remember what the Bible says, and gives us courage to talk about our church or church club to our friends.)

CREW SKILL PRACTICE

- Don't forget to use the Power Source Prayer. It not only connects you with God, but it helps the person you are praying for, too.
- How is your compliment list growing? Add two more things to it. (See pages 33–34.)
- Work on Bible Blueprint Verse 2 (page 10) and record your work points.

FRIDAY, DAY 13

CHECK THE MASTER PLAN: Read 2 Kings 5:1–15

THINK ABOUT IT: Why did the slave girl care about Naaman? It was his army that captured her and took her away from home. Maybe it was because Naaman was a good master. And maybe it was because she wanted Naaman to know that God was good. Whatever her reasons, this young girl spoke up when she had the chance to help someone. Have you ever told someone about Jesus? Do you look for chances to tell people about him? Do you really believe that God can help people with their problems? If you do, then why not tell them about Jesus?

THE CARPENTER'S PENCIL

Naaman needed cleaning up and so does the old bus below. Pretend that your church or church club bought it and it's your job to paint it. Be creative! Put special messages on it to let folks know how great your church or club is. Then tell a friend about your messages.

CREW SKILL PRACTICE

- Power up with the Power Source Prayer. (See page 1.)
- Add two more compliments to your list. Can you use the messages on your bus? (See pages 33–34.)
- Invite someone to church or church club. (Remember to talk with a parent first.)
- Record your work points.

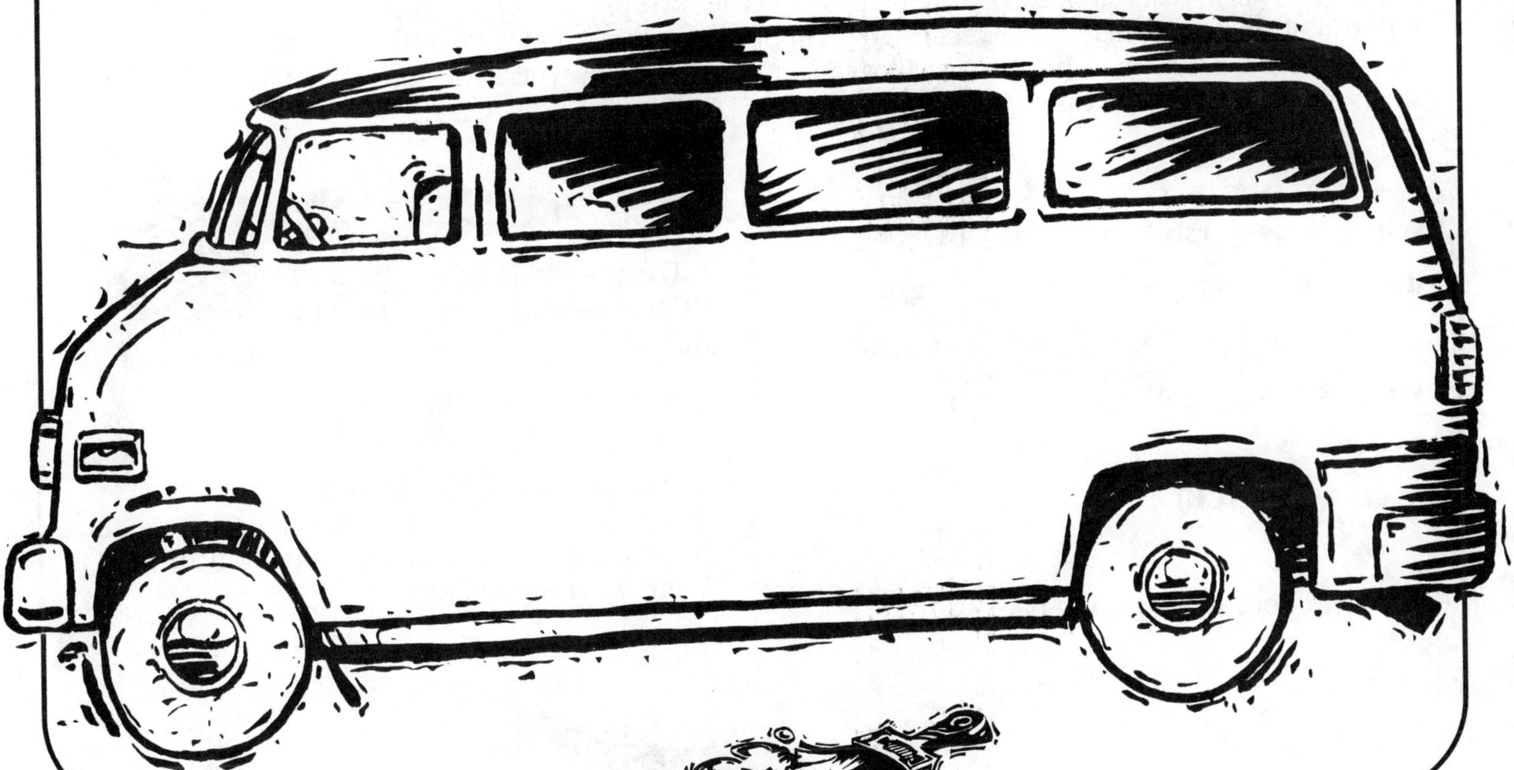

SATURDAY, DAY 14

Aaaaa
aaa
eeeee
Iiiiiii
ooooo
oooooo
uyy

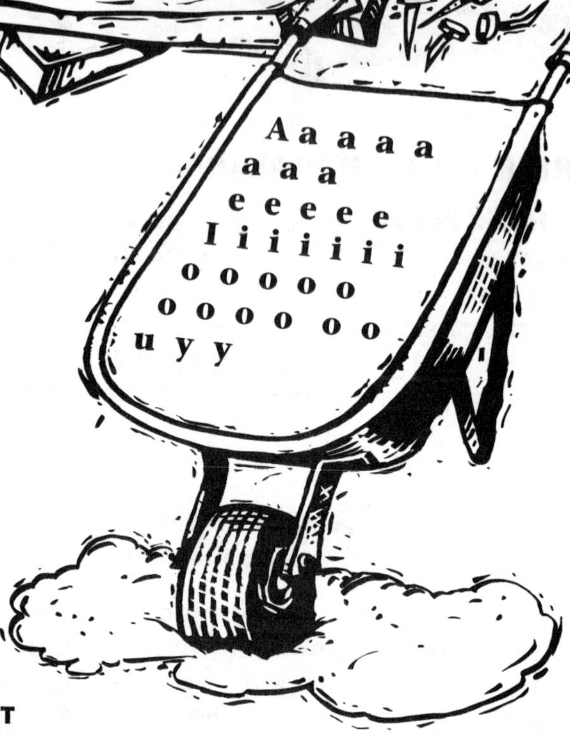

LEVEL CHECK

WEEK 3 (5 POINTS)

This is the start of Week 3 of the Adventure. How are you doing? Have you settled into a good work routine yet? So far you've inspected the way you and your church family take care of each other. You've also learned about how to say good things that will make other people want to come to your church or club. This week you'll learn about improving your friendship skills. You need to be friendly if you want to help your church or club grow.

BIBLE BLUEPRINT

VERSE CHECK

VERSE 3 (20 POINTS)

This week's verse is about opening the door to new friendships. You'll learn more about it tomorrow. But, something happened to our verse below. All of the vowels fell off, including the letter Y. The missing letters are in the wheelbarrow above. Can you figure out where they go? (Hint: Start with the small words first; they're easier to figure out.)

G _ d _ cc _ pts _ n _ _ n _
wh _ w _ rsh _ ps h _ m _ nd
d _ _ s wh _ t _ s r _ ght.
_ t _ s n _ t _ mp _ rt _ nt
wh _ t c _ _ ntr _ _ p _ rs _ n
c _ m _ s fr _ m.
_ cts 10:35 (ICB)

(To check your work, turn to page 10.)

CREW SKILL PRACTICE

- Use the Power Source Prayer. Choose a new person to pray for this week.
- Add another good comment about your church or club to your list.
- Start learning Bible Blueprint Verse 3. Record your work points. Give yourself an extra 20 points if you can say Bible Blueprint Verse 2 (page 10) from memory.

SUNDAY, DAY 15

CHECK THE MASTER PLAN: Read Acts 10:1–35

THINK ABOUT IT: Jesus gave Simon the name Peter (the rock) because his faith was as solid as concrete. But sometimes Peter was also hard-headed. It wasn't easy to change Peter's mind. How many times did God show Peter the vision of the unclean animals? ________________ (Jewish law said these animals were not to be eaten. Therefore, they were called unclean.) What did God tell Peter about the animals?

____

It was also a Jewish law not to visit Gentiles (people who were not Jewish). God used the vision to let Peter know something. What was it? (See verse 28b.)

____

Design a bumper sticker about how kids can be friends with people who are different from them.

CREW SKILL PRACTICE

• Energize with the Power Source Prayer (page 1). If you see the person you're praying for today, be sure to say hello.

• Add one more good comment about your church or club to your list. (See Crew Skill 2, page 8.) Tell a friend about your good comment.

• Work on learning Bible Blueprint Verse 3 (page 10) and record work points.

MONDAY, DAY 16

CHECK THE MASTER PLAN:
Read Leviticus 19:32–34

THINK ABOUT IT: As you just read, some things never seem to change. Ever since Moses' time, people have had to be reminded to be kind to old people and people from other countries (aliens). Why do you think that is? Why do some people make fun of old people and people from other countries? (Talk with your family about this.) God says that you

should **(OEVL)** ____________________

them as **(SLYRUOEF)** ________________
(Unscramble the words.)

These crew members came from other countries. Unscramble the letters on their signs to find out where they came from. Do you know people from places like these?

CREW SKILL PRACTICE

- Use the Power Source Prayer. Did you choose someone new to pray for this week?
- Look for a chance to be friendly to someone you don't know very well.
- Add something new to your list of 50 good things you can say about your church or church club.
- Work on Bible Blueprint Verse 3 (page 10) and record your work points.

Give yourself 5 points each time you do something loving or kind this week for someone old or from another country.

ANSWERS: PAKISTAN, KOREA, ETHIOPIA

TUESDAY, DAY 17

CHECK THE MASTER PLAN: Read James 2:1–9

THINK ABOUT IT: How are people treated at your church? Do rich and poor people get treated the same? ___________________________

Who do you think has an easier time making friends, a rich person or a poor one? _________

Why do you think that happens? __________

____

____

When rich people have problems, they often turn to their money first for help. But poor people who believe in God usually turn to him. They give God more chances to show what he can do for them. That can make them rich in

__ __ __ __ __ . (verse 5)

What really counts in a friend? Circle the six things below that you think are most important. Then try to find the words you circled in the word search puzzle.

WEALTH KINDNESS CHEERFULNESS PATIENCE HELPFULNESS POPULARITY STRENGTH FORGIVENESS RACE INTELLIGENCE NATIONALITY GODLINESS

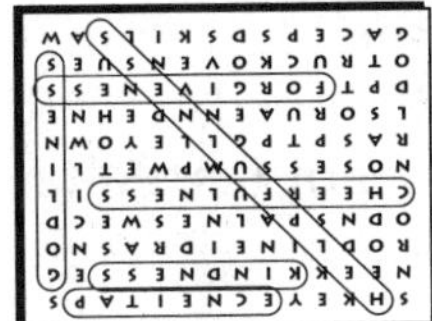

ANSWERS:

CREW SKILL PRACTICE

- Plug into the Power Source Prayer.
- Add a new item to your list of 50 compliments about your church or church club.
- Look for a way to be friendly to someone with the qualities in the puzzle.
- Work on Bible Blueprint Verse 3 (page 10) and record your work points.

S H K E Y E C N E I T A P S
N E E K K I N D N E S S E G
R O D L I N E I D R A S N O
O D N S P A L N E S W E C D
C H E E R F U L N E S S I L
N O S E S S U M P W E T L I
R A S P T P G L L E Y O W N
L S O R U A E N N D E H N E
D P T F O R G I V E N E S S
O T R U C K O V E N S U E S
G A C E P S D S K I L S A W

WEDNESDAY, DAY 18

CHECK THE MASTER PLAN:
Read Romans 14:1–12, 16–19

THINK ABOUT IT: How many churches are there in your town?

____

(Look in the yellow pages of your phone book for help.) List three kinds of churches.

____

____

____

What makes these churches different? How are they alike? (These would be good questions to talk about with your family.) What does God have to say about differences in his church crews? (Look at verses 16–19 once again.) What is really important to God?

____

____

____

CREW SKILL PRACTICE

• Plug into the Power Source Prayer.

• Add a new item to your list of 50 compliments (pages 33–34).

• Sing your crew song for a friend.

• Work on Bible Blueprint Verse 3 (page 10) and record your work points.

THE CARPENTER'S PENCIL

Most people like to hum, sing, whistle, or listen to music while they work. Try to create your own G. H. Construction Crew song. Choose a familiar tune, such as the ones listed below. Then write new lyrics (words) for it that will tell people some of the reasons you like your church or church club. (The list you started making for Crew Skill 2 may help give you ideas.) Check with your family to see if you can invite a friend over to help you. Use notebook paper since you'll need lots of room to write.

(Song Choices: "He's Got the Whole World in His Hands," "Row, Row, Row Your Boat," "The Bear Went Over the Mountain," "I've Been Working on the Railroad," "O Christmas Tree," and "O Little Town of Bethlehem.")

THURSDAY, DAY 19

CHECK THE MASTER PLAN:
Read Acts 9:19b–31

THINK ABOUT IT: Is it possible for someone who is known for doing bad things to become a good person? Yes, it happened to the apostle Paul (who was known as Saul back then). Paul thought he was doing the right thing when he chased down Christians and had them stoned or put in jail. He was wrong. And God told him so. Paul became a believer in Jesus and one of the very first Christian missionaries. Paul's life story might have been very different if those early Christians hadn't forgiven Paul and believed that he was a changed man. We all need God to help us change things in our lives, too. Is God showing you something you need to change? Write about it.

____

____

____

____

____

CREW SKILL PRACTICE

- Plug into the Power Source Prayer (page 1).
- Add a new item to your list of 50 compliments.
- Work on Bible Blueprint Verse 3 (page 10) and record your work points.

THE CARPENTER'S PENCIL

Paul made a big change. He went from being mean to Christians to being kind. Can you change the word MEAN into the word KIND by changing one letter at a time? The numbered clues on the left should help. (Answer key below.)

M	E	A	N
K	I	N	D

1. Not at all fat

2. A heavy metal

3. To loan something

4. A turn in the road

5. To tie with rope or string

Who have you been kind to lately?

____

____

____

ANSWERS: MEAN, LEAN, LEAD, LEND, BEND, BIND, KIND

HERE'S WHY MY CHURCH IS GREAT!

LIST 50 GOOD THINGS ABOUT YOUR CHURCH OR CHURCH CLUB HERE.

1. ______________________________
2. ______________________________
3. ______________________________
4. ______________________________
5. ______________________________
6. ______________________________
7. ______________________________
8. ______________________________
9. ______________________________
10. ______________________________
11. ______________________________
12. ______________________________
13. ______________________________
14. ______________________________
15. ______________________________
16. ______________________________
17. ______________________________
18. ______________________________
19. ______________________________
20. ______________________________
21. ______________________________
22. ______________________________

23. ______________________________

24. ______________________________

25. ______________________________

26. ______________________________

27. ______________________________

28. ______________________________

29. ______________________________

30. ______________________________

31. ______________________________

32. ______________________________

33. ______________________________

34. ______________________________

35. ______________________________

36. ______________________________

37. ______________________________

38. ______________________________

39. ______________________________

40. ______________________________

41. ______________________________

42. ______________________________

43. ______________________________

44. ______________________________

45. ______________________________

46. ______________________________

47. ______________________________

48. ______________________________

49. ______________________________

50. ______________________________

FRIDAY, DAY 20

CHECK THE MASTER PLAN:
Read Revelation 7:9–10

THINK ABOUT IT: What you just read is a small part of the vision the apostle John had of heaven. With God's help he wrote about it in the Book of Revelation. Someday everyone who is a part of God's crew (the family of God) will gather around God's throne to praise him. It will be one grand celebration! And the faces in the crowd will come from every nation and race.

You can get an idea of what heaven will be like by getting to know people who are different from you. One way is to be friendly to people who come from other countries. Can you think of another way you can show people who are different from you that God loves them?

____

____

CREW SKILL PRACTICE

- Don't forget to power up with prayer (page 1).
- Have you made a new friend yet? Invite someone new in your neighborhood or your school to eat lunch with you.
- Add one more good comment to your list of compliments (Crew Skill 2, page 8).
- Work on Bible Blueprint Verse 3 (page 10) and record your work points.

Can you find the 10 faces hidden in this scene? Color them to represent people of all skin colors. How might these people be like you? And how might they be different?

Saturday, Day 21

LEVEL CHECK

WEEK 4 (5 POINTS)

How did things go this past week? Were you able to start a new friendship? If not, don't worry. Building a new friendship can take time. So keep trying. And if you have been able to start a new friendship, work at making it a good one. Today is the first day of Week 4. The activities this week will help you appreciate your talents as well as the talents of others. And they will get you thinking about how you can serve God. Take some time today to review Crew Skill 4 on page 9.

CREW SKILL PRACTICE

- It's time to choose a new person to pray for in your Power Source Prayers this week.
- Volunteer to do something helpful at home.
- Add a good comment to your list of 50 nice things you can say about your church or church club (pages 33–34).
- Work on Bible Blueprint Verse 4 (page 10) and record your work points.

BIBLE BLUEPRINT

VERSE CHECK

VERSE 4 (10 POINTS)

Turn to page 10 to find this week's verse. Mark the page with a paper clip or a bookmark. Then turn back here. Color all the spaces in the puzzle that have words on them found in this week's verse from 1 Peter 4:10a. (Hint: The words will not be in order, and some may appear more than once.) When you are done, you should find a symbol of one gift God wants everyone both to have and to give away.

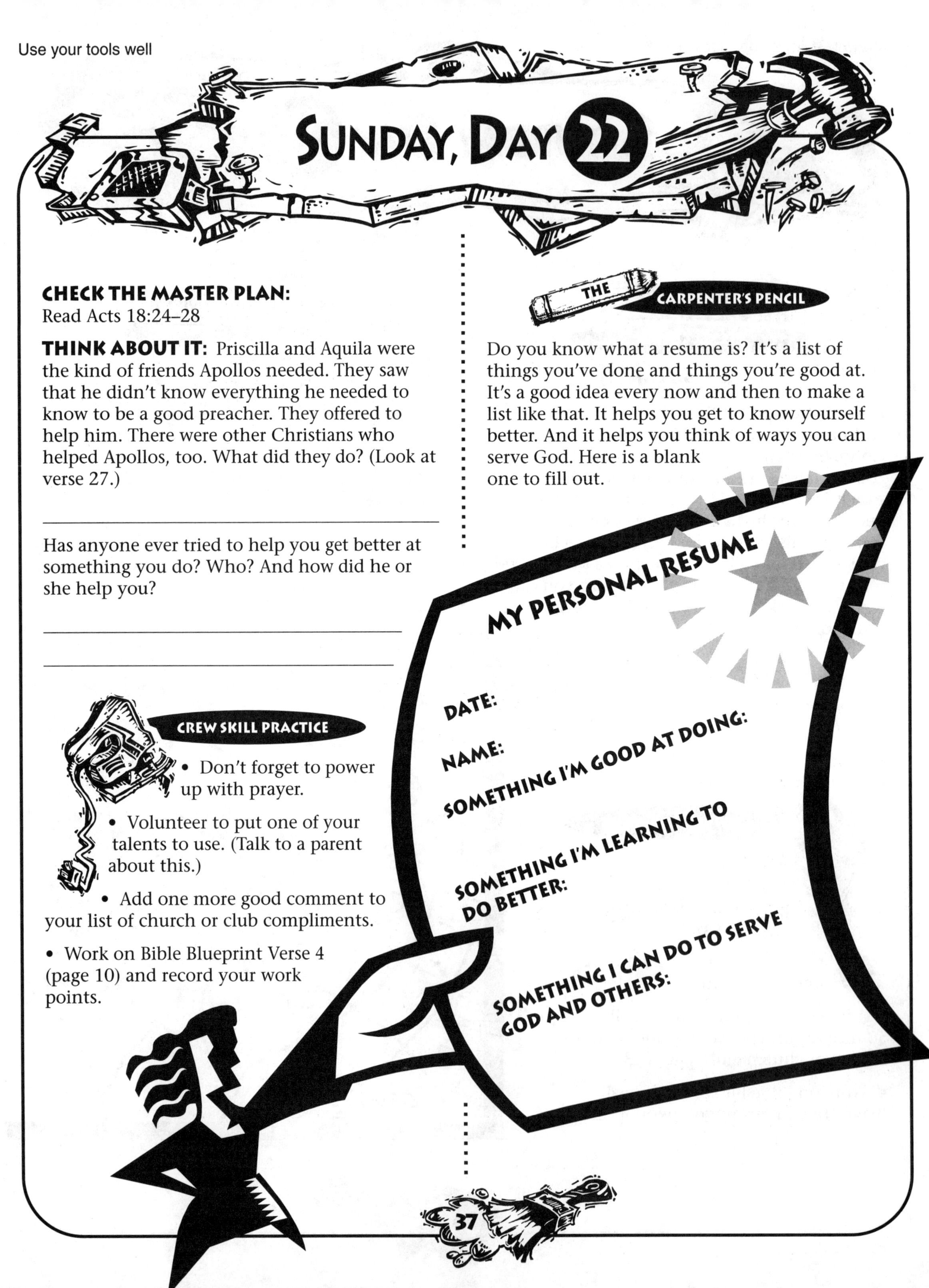

SUNDAY, DAY 22

CHECK THE MASTER PLAN:
Read Acts 18:24–28

THINK ABOUT IT: Priscilla and Aquila were the kind of friends Apollos needed. They saw that he didn't know everything he needed to know to be a good preacher. They offered to help him. There were other Christians who helped Apollos, too. What did they do? (Look at verse 27.)

____

Has anyone ever tried to help you get better at something you do? Who? And how did he or she help you?

____

____

CREW SKILL PRACTICE

- Don't forget to power up with prayer.
- Volunteer to put one of your talents to use. (Talk to a parent about this.)
- Add one more good comment to your list of church or club compliments.
- Work on Bible Blueprint Verse 4 (page 10) and record your work points.

THE CARPENTER'S PENCIL

Do you know what a resume is? It's a list of things you've done and things you're good at. It's a good idea every now and then to make a list like that. It helps you get to know yourself better. And it helps you think of ways you can serve God. Here is a blank one to fill out.

MY PERSONAL RESUME

DATE:

NAME:

SOMETHING I'M GOOD AT DOING:

SOMETHING I'M LEARNING TO DO BETTER:

SOMETHING I CAN DO TO SERVE GOD AND OTHERS:

MONDAY, DAY 23

CHECK THE MASTER PLAN:
Read Matthew 9:9–13

THINK ABOUT IT: Jesus was good at picking the right person for the right job. He saw things in people that others didn't. The religious leaders of Jesus' day looked down on tax collectors like Matthew. They saw them as dishonest men. But Jesus believed Matthew could change and use his talents for good. For example, as a tax collector Matthew learned to keep good records and write well. This made him a good man to write the first book of the New Testament. What is a talent or ability you can use to serve God?

CREW SKILL PRACTICE

- Plug into the Power Source Prayer (page 1).
- Compliment someone for something he or she did well.
- Add something about your church or your church club to your list of 50 compliments (pages 33–34). Tell a friend about one of your compliments.
- Work on Bible Blueprint Verse 4 (page 10) and record your work points.

THE CARPENTER'S PENCIL

Jesus' twelve disciples were just ordinary guys. But because he believed in them, all but one climbed the ladder to true success. Almost 2000 years later, people are still talking about them. Try to fit the disciples' names into the puzzle. (Don't worry about the names in parentheses. They're like nicknames.)

TUESDAY, DAY 24

CHECK THE MASTER PLAN: Read Philemon (Yes, the whole book!)

THINK ABOUT IT: Talk about old mail! You just read a letter that was written almost 2000 years ago. Fill in the blanks using these names: Philemon, Onesimus, and Paul. Look back at the verses you read if you need help.

The apostle Paul wrote to help make peace between two of his friends, ___________ and ___________. ___________ was ___________'s run-away servant. The letter doesn't say exactly what ___________ did wrong before he ran away, but it shows he was worried about it. While he was on the run, ___________ met _____ and became a Christian. _____ knew that ___________ needed to set things right with ___________ before he could be a faithful servant of God. So Paul talked ___________ into returning home to ask for forgiveness. And as a good friend, _____ wrote this letter to ask ___________ to forgive ___________ and welcome him home.

Have you ever stuck up for someone and acted as a peacemaker? Or has someone stuck up for you? Draw a picture of what happened.

ANSWERS: PHILEMON, ONESIMUS, ONESIMUS, PHILEMON, ONESIMUS, ONESIMUS, PAUL, PAUL, ONESIMUS, PHILEMON, ONESIMUS, PAUL, PHILEMON, ONESIMUS

CREW SKILL PRACTICE

- Plug into the Power Source Prayer.
- Compliment someone for something he or she did well. That's a good way to stick up for a person.
- Add something new to the list of nice things you're saying about your church or club. How many do you have so far?
- Work on Bible Blueprint Verse 4 (page 10) and record your work points.

(30 Bonus Points)

Offer your services to someone at home. Try to do everything you are asked without grumbling. This is one way to put your abilities to use. Do the best job you can.

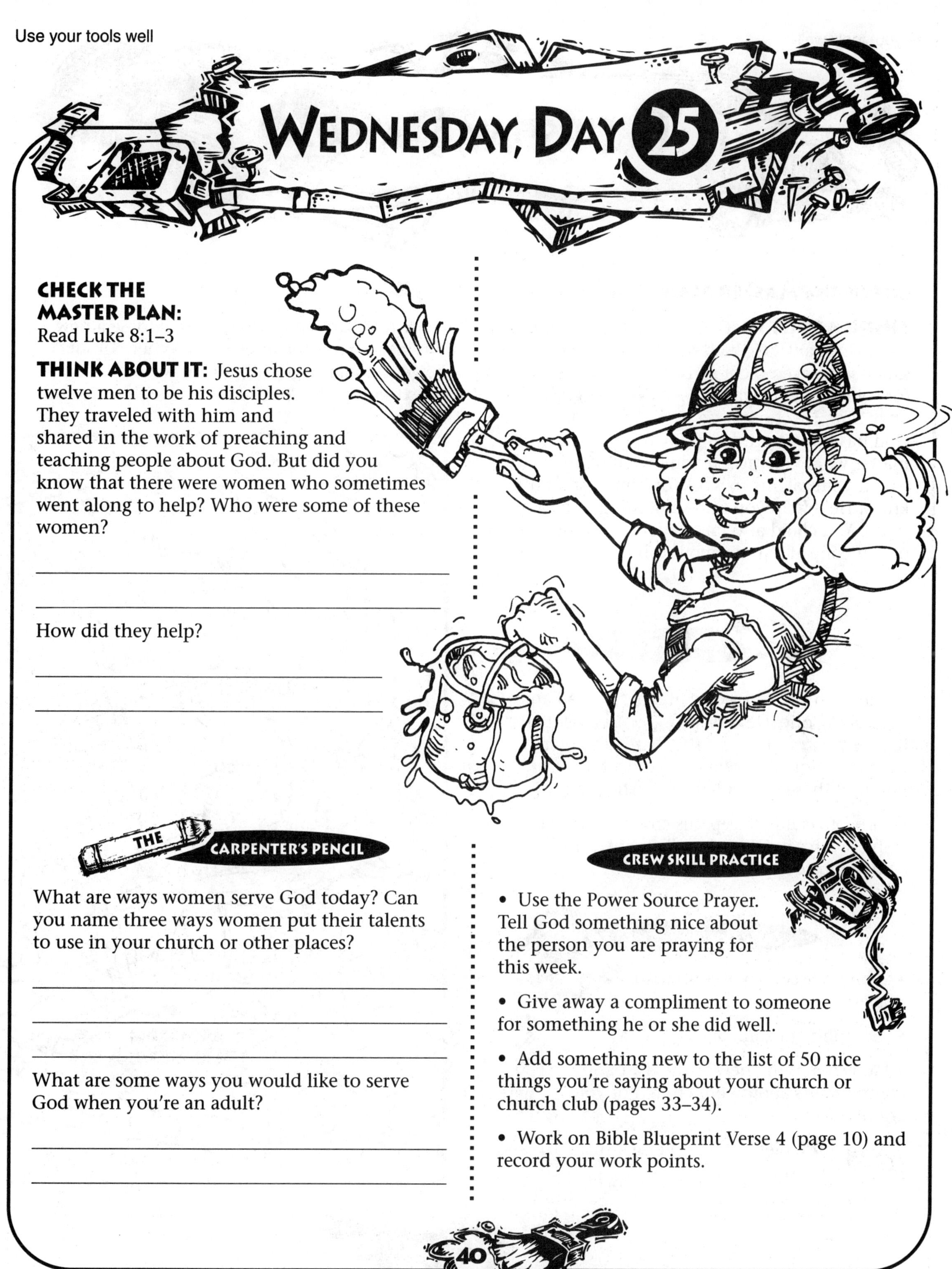

WEDNESDAY, DAY 25

CHECK THE MASTER PLAN:
Read Luke 8:1–3

THINK ABOUT IT: Jesus chose twelve men to be his disciples. They traveled with him and shared in the work of preaching and teaching people about God. But did you know that there were women who sometimes went along to help? Who were some of these women?

____

____

How did they help?

____

____

THE CARPENTER'S PENCIL

What are ways women serve God today? Can you name three ways women put their talents to use in your church or other places?

____

____

____

What are some ways you would like to serve God when you're an adult?

____

____

CREW SKILL PRACTICE

- Use the Power Source Prayer. Tell God something nice about the person you are praying for this week.
- Give away a compliment to someone for something he or she did well.
- Add something new to the list of 50 nice things you're saying about your church or church club (pages 33–34).
- Work on Bible Blueprint Verse 4 (page 10) and record your work points.

THURSDAY, DAY 26

CHECK THE MASTER PLAN: Read 1 Samuel 16:1–13

THINK ABOUT IT: God was disappointed in King Saul. He told Samuel it was time to choose a new king. God said, "Go to Jesse's home. I've chosen one of his sons to be king after Saul." When Samuel saw Jesse's seven older sons, he was impressed. They were good-looking guys. But God wasn't looking for someone who was just good-looking. He wanted the next king to be someone who would love and obey him. He chose Jesse's youngest son, David. God has important things for you to do, too, no matter what your age. If you love him and want to put your talents to work for him, just let him know. He'll help you find something important to do. You could also talk to your mom or dad or someone at church about this.

THE CARPENTER'S PENCIL

David didn't have an easy life, but he had an interesting one. He served God with his talents in many ways. He was a shepherd, a soldier, a harpist, a singer, a composer, and a king. Can you find these things hidden in the picture?

> one of David's sheep, his crown, his spear, his sword, his harp, his slingshot, and two music notes (eighth notes)

CREW SKILL PRACTICE

- Don't forget to power up with prayer.
- Compliment someone else today.
- Add something new to the list of 50 compliments about your church or your church club.
- Work on Bible Blueprint Verse 4 (page 10) and record your work points.

FRIDAY, DAY 27

CHECK THE MASTER PLAN: Read Acts 4:1–14

THINK ABOUT IT: Look your best! Feel your best! Be all you can be! These are the messages we hear every day. It seems like almost everyone has an idea about how we can become new and improved. But no one has had more success turning ordinary people into extraordinary people than Jesus has. Just look at what he did with Peter and John, the two fishermen in our story. He gave them the power to heal the sick and to preach the Scriptures with courage and understanding.

THE CARPENTER'S PENCIL

Have you ever been afraid to serve God because you didn't think you could cut through the difficulties? Well, the apostle Paul has this message for you. To decode it, start with the circled letter **"I."** Then write every other letter on the lines provided. You should be done in two clockwise spins of the saw blade.

I ___ ___ ___ ___ ___

___ ___ ___ ___ ___ ___ ___ ___ ___ ___

___ ___ ___ ___ ___ ___ ___ ___ ___ ___ ___

___ ___ ___ **GIVES ME STRENGTH.**

Philippians 4:13

ANSWERS: I CAN DO EVERYTHING THROUGH HIM WHO GIVES ME STRENGTH.

CREW SKILL PRACTICE

- Power up with prayer.
- Compliment yourself for a talent or ability God has given you. Ask your mom or dad or someone else to compliment you, too!
- Add something new to the list of 50 church or church club compliments.
- Tell a friend about one of your church compliments.
- Work on Bible Blueprint Verse 4 (page 10) and record your work points.

Saturday, Day 28

LEVEL CHECK

WEEK 5 (5 POINTS)

You're more than halfway through the Adventure now. Has praying for people and trying to make new friendships helped you feel closer to your church family? Has looking for good things to say about your church made you appreciate it more? What did you learn about using your talents to serve God?

Are you ready for your next Crew Skill? Then you're ready to do a bit of cleaning. Turn back to page 10 and review Crew Skill 5. (Mark the page because you'll be turning back there again.)

If you want to be "a worker who is not ashamed of his work," grab a broom and a dustpan. It's time to start cleaning. (Actually you'll need three sheets of paper and a pencil to make your "Things to Clean Out" lists.) Use these three titles for the pages of your lists: 1. Garbage Fun, 2. Trashy Talk, 3. Junky Thoughts. Then ask yourself the question, "If I could see Jesus standing next to me, would I do, say, or think this?" If not, describe what you wouldn't do, say, or think on the appropriate list. Hang on to your lists all week long and add to them as you find new bits of "trash" in your life. Ask God to help you make the necessary changes. Then next Saturday, tear up the lists and throw them away. (Remember, just like you have to continually clean up your room, you will need to continually clean out the "trash" in your life, too.)

BIBLE BLUEPRINT VERSE CHECK

VERSE 5 (10 POINTS)

The Bible Blueprint Verse for Week 5 is found on page 10. (Aren't you glad you marked the page?) To help you practice this memory verse, write each word on a separate note card or slip of paper. Mix the cards and then time yourself to see how quickly you can put them in order again. When you think you are starting to learn the verse, test yourself by removing two or three cards. Then see if you can put the cards in order and say the missing words.

CREW SKILL PRACTICE

- Remember to ask for forgiveness for the "trash" you write on your "Things to Clean Out" lists this week in your Power Source Prayers.
- Add a church compliment to your list on pages 33–34.
- Work on learning Bible Blueprint Verse 5 (page 10) and record your work points.

Take out the trash

CHECK THE MASTER PLAN:
Read Acts 20:32–38

THINK ABOUT IT: In these verses Paul was telling his friends good-bye. But he also wanted to teach them one more time about the right attitudes God wanted them to have. We can use verses like these to measure how we're growing in our Christian lives. Can you name three things Paul mentioned?

____

____

____

CREW SKILL PRACTICE

- Power up with prayer and tell God about any bad attitudes you may have.
- Add a church compliment to your list.
- Add items to your "Things to Clean Out" lists. (See page 43.)
- Work on learning Bible Blueprint Verse 5 (page 10) and record your work points.

(10 BONUS POINTS)

Carpenters know that measuring is important, too. Here are two projects to help you practice your measuring skills.

PROJECT A

1. Cut a sheet of ruled notebook paper into 13 strips. (Cut along the ruled lines.)
2. Number the strips on one end, then cut Strip 1 in half.
3. Use Strip 1 as a measuring tool to cut the rest of the strips the same length.
4. When all the strips are cut, compare Strip 1 and Strip 13. Are they the same length?

PROJECT B

1. Repeat Steps 1–3 of Project A. But now each time you cut a strip, use it as the measuring tool for the next strip.
2. Compare Strip 1 and Strip 13. Are they the same length?

Which measuring project gave you the best result?

Why?

(Answer key below.)

ANSWER: PROJECT A-yes. **PROJECT B**-no. **PROJECT A** worked best because the same measuring tool (Strip 1) was used to measure each of the other strips. In **PROJECT B** the measuring tool changed each time a new strip was cut. This caused the strips to be cut a little longer each time. Does this help you understand why God gave us one set standard (the Bible) to measure our behavior? Without this unchanging measuring tool, we might start calling good things bad and bad things good.

MONDAY, DAY 30

CHECK THE MASTER PLAN:
Read Mark 11:15–17

THINK ABOUT IT: When Jesus came to the city of Jerusalem for the last time, he came knowing that he would die soon. But before he died, he wanted to clean out the temple (God's House). It was full of people getting rich by making poor people pay high prices to buy animals for sacrifices. Sometimes we do or think the wrong kinds of things, too. Jesus wants to help us clean things out. What do you need help cleaning out of your heart and mind? Mean thoughts toward others? Jealousy? Unforgiveness? The words you use?

CREW SKILL PRACTICE

- Power up with prayer and ask God to help you choose your words more carefully.
- Add another compliment to your list. Tell a friend what you wrote.
- Is there anything you need to add to your "Things to Clean Out" lists? (See page 43.)
- Work on Bible Blueprint Verse 5 (page 10) and record your work points.

ANSWERS: I HOPE MY WORDS AND THOUGHTS PLEASE YOU. (LORD)

Jesus chose his words carefully, even when he was angry. He didn't swear or use God's name the wrong way. He didn't use words to get even with people or to hurt them.

Decode the Bible verse and then think about these questions: Could you say these words and mean them? Or would you have to make some changes first?

A	B	C	D	E	F	G	H	I	J	K	L	M
1	2	3	4	5	6	7	8	9	10	11	12	13
N	**O**	**P**	**Q**	**R**	**S**	**T**	**U**	**V**	**W**	**X**	**Y**	**Z**
14	15	16	17	18	19	20	21	22	23	24	25	26

__ (9)   __ __ __ __ (8 15 16 5)   __ __ (13 25)

__ __ __ __ __ (23 15 18 4 19)   __ __ __ (1 14 4)

__ __ __ __ __ __ __ __ (20 8 15 21 7 8 20 19)

__ __ __ __ __ __ (16 12 5 1 19 5)

__ __ __ (25 15 21). (Lord)

Psalm 19:14a (ICB)

Take out the trash

TUESDAY, DAY 31

CHECK THE MASTER PLAN: Read Psalm 15

THINK ABOUT IT: When a person builds a building, he or she wants it to be built using the best materials so it will be strong. In Psalm 15 King David describes some of the things God, the Master Builder, wants us to use to build our lives.

THE CARPENTER'S PENCIL

Look over Psalm 15 again. On the chart below, list the things we should do and the things we shouldn't do. Then put a red check beside the things you need to work on in order to build a strong Christian life.

BLUEPRINTS FOR A PERSON OF INTEGRITY

THINGS WE SHOULD DO	THINGS WE SHOULDN'T DO

CREW SKILL PRACTICE

- Use the Power Source Prayer. Tell God something nice about the person you're praying for this week.
- Add another compliment to your list of 50 on pages 33–34. How many do you have?
- Work on Bible Blueprint Verse 5 (page 10) and record your work points.

WEDNESDAY, DAY 32

CHECK THE MASTER PLAN:
Read Genesis 35:1–5

THINK ABOUT IT: When you mix together cement, gravel, and water in the right amounts, you create concrete, a strong, rock-solid building material. But not all things are good to mix together. Some mixtures are just mixed-up messes. And a mixed-up mess is what Jacob had. His wives, his sons, their wives, and everybody's servants had mixed up worshiping God with worshiping idols. Jacob knew that before he and his family moved to a new place, they needed to clean out their hearts by giving up their idols. They needed to worship God only. What did they do with their idols?

____

Do you have anything you put your trust in instead of God? (For example: What your friends think, a lucky coin, and so on) What is it? And what should you do about it?

____

CREW SKILL PRACTICE

- Plug into the Power Source Prayer.
- Add another compliment to your list of 50. Share one or two with a friend.
- To be "a worker who is not ashamed of his work," you need to take out the trash in your life. Do you need to add anything to your "Things to Clean Out" lists?
- Work on Bible Blueprint Verse 5 and record your work points.

How are you doing with this week's Bible Blueprint Verse? Try finding it in the word mixture below by crossing out the extra ingredients. (Turn to page 10 to check your work.)

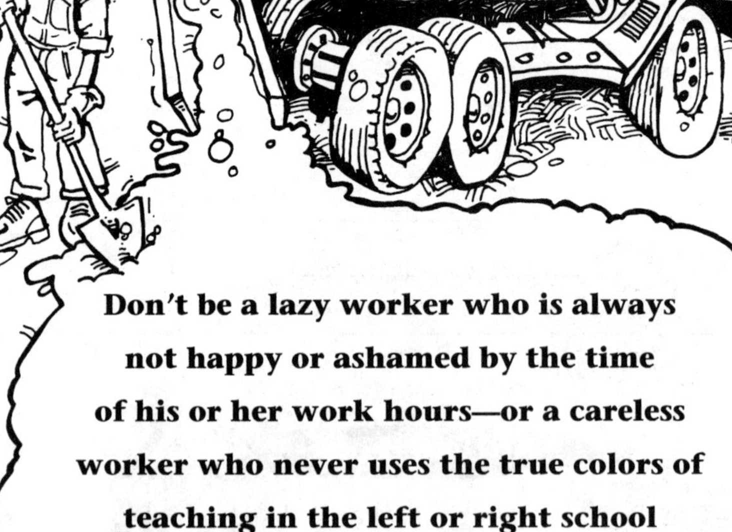

Don't be a lazy worker who is always not happy or ashamed by the time of his or her work hours—or a careless worker who never uses the true colors of teaching in the left or right school hallway way.

12 Thomas Timothy 42:115abc

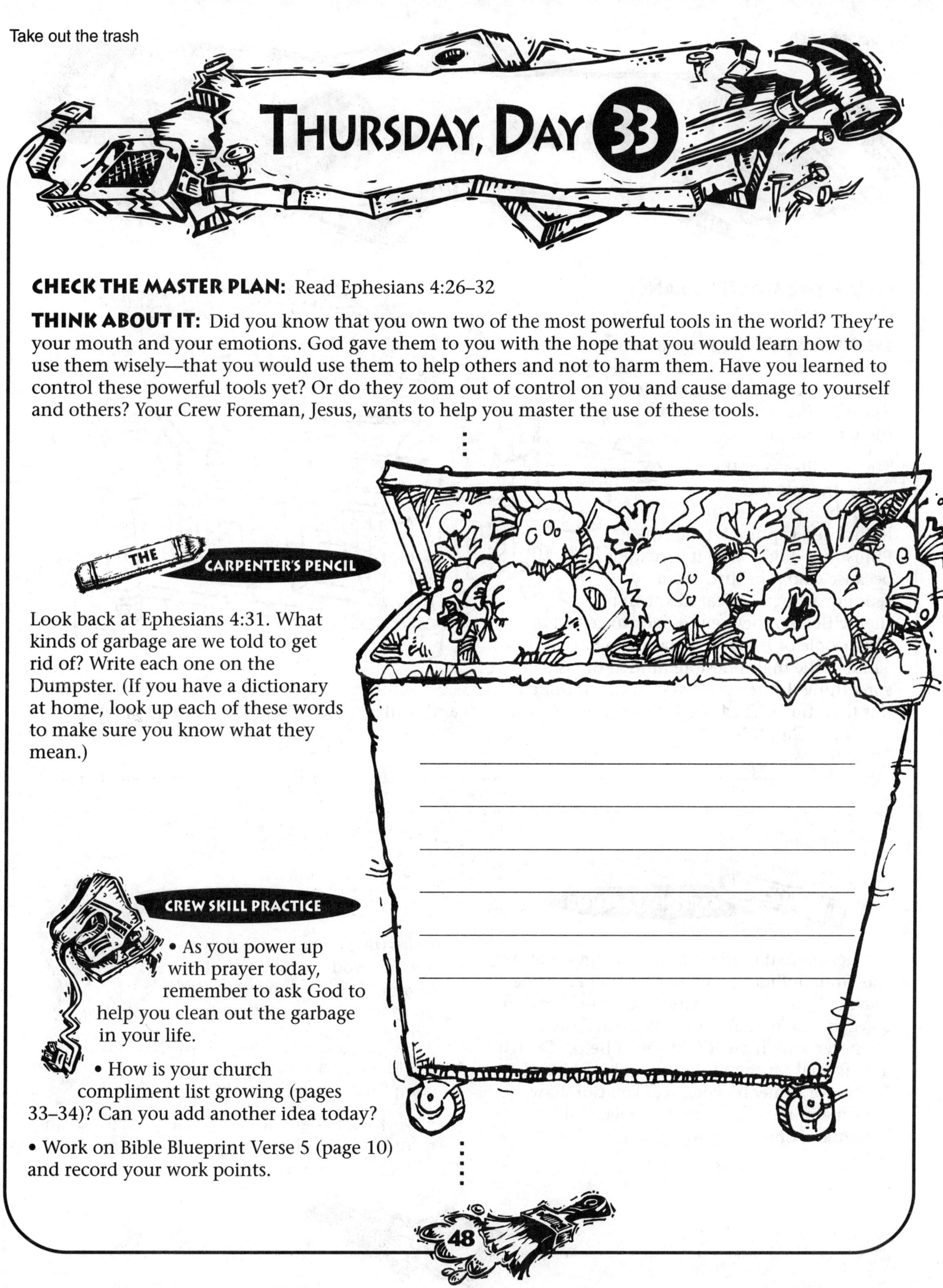

Thursday, Day 33

CHECK THE MASTER PLAN: Read Ephesians 4:26–32

THINK ABOUT IT: Did you know that you own two of the most powerful tools in the world? They're your mouth and your emotions. God gave them to you with the hope that you would learn how to use them wisely—that you would use them to help others and not to harm them. Have you learned to control these powerful tools yet? Or do they zoom out of control on you and cause damage to yourself and others? Your Crew Foreman, Jesus, wants to help you master the use of these tools.

THE CARPENTER'S PENCIL

Look back at Ephesians 4:31. What kinds of garbage are we told to get rid of? Write each one on the Dumpster. (If you have a dictionary at home, look up each of these words to make sure you know what they mean.)

CREW SKILL PRACTICE

• As you power up with prayer today, remember to ask God to help you clean out the garbage in your life.

• How is your church compliment list growing (pages 33–34)? Can you add another idea today?

• Work on Bible Blueprint Verse 5 (page 10) and record your work points.

FRIDAY, DAY 34

CHECK THE MASTER PLAN:
Read 1 Samuel 7:2–13

THINK ABOUT IT: Do you remember what the Ark of the Covenant is? It's the special storage box Moses had made for the Ten Commandments and the jar of manna.

The Israelites kept the ark in the tabernacle until their enemies, the Philistines, captured it. But the Philistines didn't keep it very long, because God punished them by sending a plague (great sickness) to their cities. So they sent it back to get rid of it. The people of Israel were happy to have it. But Samuel, the high priest, reminded the Israelites of something. If they wanted God to continue to protect them from their enemies, they needed to take out their trash. They needed to get rid of their idols and confess their sins to God. What happened when they did this?

____

____

Samuel wanted to remind the Israelites that it was God, not idols, who helped them in times of trouble. So he had a large rock set on end to serve as a memorial stone. He named the stone Ebenezer, which means "stone of help." Design a memorial for something special God has done for you or someone you love. You can draw your memorial on a sheet of paper, make a bookmark, or use clay to shape it.

CREW SKILL PRACTICE

- Use the Power Source Prayer and ask God to show you the idols and sins you need to clean up in your life. Add them to your list. (See page 43.)
- Add another idea to your church compliment list.
- Work on Bible Blueprint Verse 5 (page 10) and record your work points.

Saturday, Day 35

Level Check

Week 6 (5 Points)

How are you doing? Did you get a good start this past week on cleaning up any garbage thoughts, words, or habits in your life? Throw away your "Things to Clean Out" lists today after praying about what you wrote. This is a symbol that you want to clean out the "trash" in your life. Remember, you will need to clean out the "trash" on a regular basis.

Today is also the start of a new theme—Help in other places. The Bible has a lot to say about what God wants his crew members to do for him in the world. So make sure you set aside some time to check it out.

1-B, 2-C, 3-D, 4-F, 5-G, 6-H, 7-K, 8-L, 9-N, 10-R, 11-S, 12-T, 13-W

YOUE EUOE OEOE EAOE OUOE EUYOYO UEOEOUE AAA

Crew Skill Practice

- Choose a new person to pray for in your Power Source Prayers this week.
- Did you remember to throw away your "Things to Clean Out" lists?
- Add a church compliment to your list (pages 33–34).
- Start learning Bible Blueprint Verse 6 (page 10) and record your work points.

Bible Blueprint Verse Check

Verse 6 (10 Points)

This week's Bible Blueprint Verse tells two ways God wanted the people of Israel to help others. The activity has two parts, like the verse.

Part 1. Use the letter key in the first dump truck on the left to fill in the missing consonants.

Part 2. Use the vowels in the other dump truck to finish the verse.

__ __ __   11 6 __ __ 8 3

4 __ __ 3   12 6 __ 11 __   13 6 __

__ 10 __   6 __ 9 5 10 __.   __ __ __

__ __ __   11 6 __ __ 8 3   12 __ 7 __

2 __ 10 __   __ 4

12 6 __   9 __ __ 3 11   __ 4

12 6 __ 11 __   13 6 __   __ 10 __

12 10 __ __ 1 8 __ 3.

Isaiah 58:10a (ICB)

(To check your work turn to page 10.)

CHECK THE MASTER PLAN:
Read Acts 16:6–15

THINK ABOUT IT: The apostle Paul's work shoes were sandals, well-worn sandals. He walked hundreds of miles to tell people about Jesus. In the story you just read, Lydia became his first European convert (believer in Jesus). Lydia was a business woman. She sold expensive purple cloth. The purple dye used to make this cloth was very rare. So only rich people could afford to wear clothing this color. (Now you know why purple is called a royal color.) Lydia wasn't content with just believing in Jesus herself. She wanted everyone in her household to believe, too. And they did! Paul went to other countries to tell people about Jesus, but Lydia went to her home. Maybe someday God will ask you to travel the world as a missionary, but for now, home is your mission field. Who can you tell about Jesus—a family member, a friend, a neighbor? Ask God to show you. Maybe you could invite that person to church or church club.

CREW SKILL PRACTICE

- Ask God how you can help in other places in your Power Source Prayers this week.
- Add a church compliment to your list. Do you have 36 yet?
- Work on learning Bible Blueprint Verse 6 (page 10).
- Talk to a friend about Jesus sometime this week, or invite that person to church or church club.
- Record your work points.

Help Paul find his way to Lydia, and then help Lydia find her way home.

Because of believers like Paul and Lydia, the good news about Jesus spread from person to person, from city to city, and then from country to country.

CHECK THE MASTER PLAN:
Read Matthew 25:31–40

THINK ABOUT IT: The words you just read are printed in red in some Bibles. That's because they are Jesus' own words. He says that someday he will sit on the throne of heaven and act as the world's judge. He will divide us into two groups. What does he call the people he will tell to stand on his left side?____________________

What does he call the people he will tell to stand on his right side? ____________________

How will he decide which group's people belong in heaven? ________________________________

____

Which group do you want to be in? __________

Why? ____________________________________

____

Jesus says he can tell his true followers by the way they treat others. His followers use their time, money, and talents to help people in need. Does this sound like you? If not, what do you need to change?

CREW SKILL PRACTICE

- Don't forget the Power Source Prayer today.
- Add a church compliment to your list. It's OK to share ideas with others.
- Work on Bible Blueprint Verse 6 (page 10) and record your work points.

Goats just *butt* problems around instead of tackling them—*but* I'm too busy to help, *but* I want to do something else, *but* that's not my problem. Think like a sheep instead. How can you use your time, money, and talents to help other people?

TUESDAY, DAY 38

CHECK THE MASTER PLAN:
Read Genesis 1:28–31

THINK ABOUT IT: When he made the earth, God created a beautiful place for us to live. He gave us plants, animals, and food. His directions for Adam and Eve were to rule over the earth. What do you think this means?

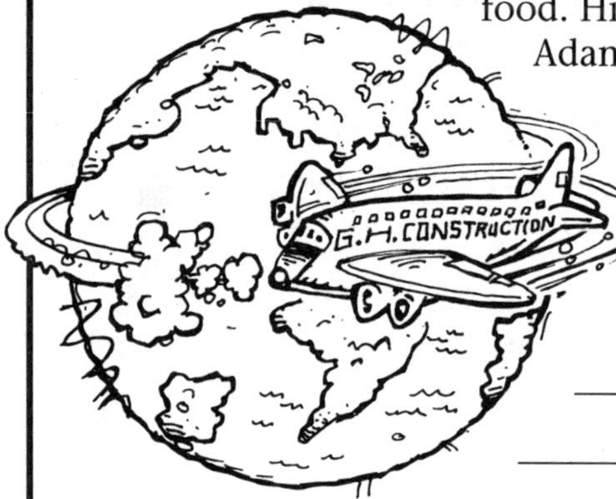

How can people take care of the earth God gave them?

Now list some ways people are harming the earth.

THE CARPENTER'S PENCIL

Of all the things God created in the world, what do you think is the most beautiful? Draw a picture of it.

What can you do to take care of it?

CREW SKILL PRACTICE

- Plug into the Power Source Prayer.
- Add a compliment to your list.
- Work on Bible Blueprint Verse 6 (page 10).
- Look for a chance to tell someone about Jesus. Or invite that person to church or church club.
- Record your work points. (It's OK to go back and do pages you missed if you want to earn some more points.)

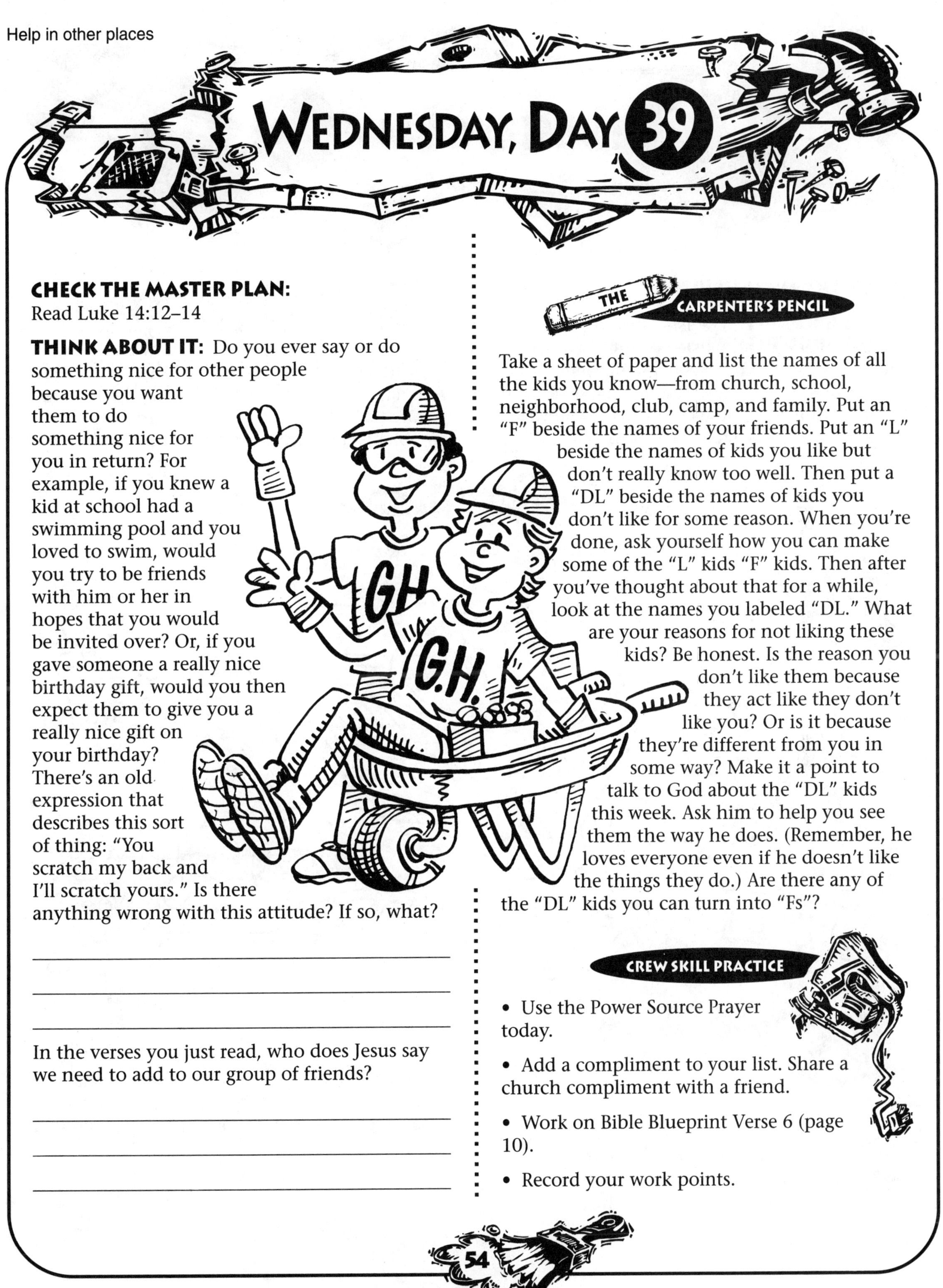

Wednesday, Day 39

CHECK THE MASTER PLAN:
Read Luke 14:12–14

THINK ABOUT IT: Do you ever say or do something nice for other people because you want them to do something nice for you in return? For example, if you knew a kid at school had a swimming pool and you loved to swim, would you try to be friends with him or her in hopes that you would be invited over? Or, if you gave someone a really nice birthday gift, would you then expect them to give you a really nice gift on your birthday? There's an old expression that describes this sort of thing: "You scratch my back and I'll scratch yours." Is there anything wrong with this attitude? If so, what?

____

____

____

In the verses you just read, who does Jesus say we need to add to our group of friends?

____

____

____

The Carpenter's Pencil

Take a sheet of paper and list the names of all the kids you know—from church, school, neighborhood, club, camp, and family. Put an "F" beside the names of your friends. Put an "L" beside the names of kids you like but don't really know too well. Then put a "DL" beside the names of kids you don't like for some reason. When you're done, ask yourself how you can make some of the "L" kids "F" kids. Then after you've thought about that for a while, look at the names you labeled "DL." What are your reasons for not liking these kids? Be honest. Is the reason you don't like them because they act like they don't like you? Or is it because they're different from you in some way? Make it a point to talk to God about the "DL" kids this week. Ask him to help you see them the way he does. (Remember, he loves everyone even if he doesn't like the things they do.) Are there any of the "DL" kids you can turn into "Fs"?

Crew Skill Practice

- Use the Power Source Prayer today.
- Add a compliment to your list. Share a church compliment with a friend.
- Work on Bible Blueprint Verse 6 (page 10).
- Record your work points.

CHECK THE MASTER PLAN: Read Isaiah 58:6–11

THINK ABOUT IT: The Israelites were proud of themselves. They went to worship every week, brought offerings, and fasted (went without eating) at special times. They did this to show God how much they wanted his blessings and help. But God was unimpressed. What he wanted them to do was to be kind to people, feed the hungry, give the homeless a place to live, clothe the poor, and take care of their families. Theses verses from Isaiah were written more than 2500 years ago. The problems God wanted his people to take care of then are a lot like the problems he wants us to take care of today.

Can you help the crew members below find the people who need their help?

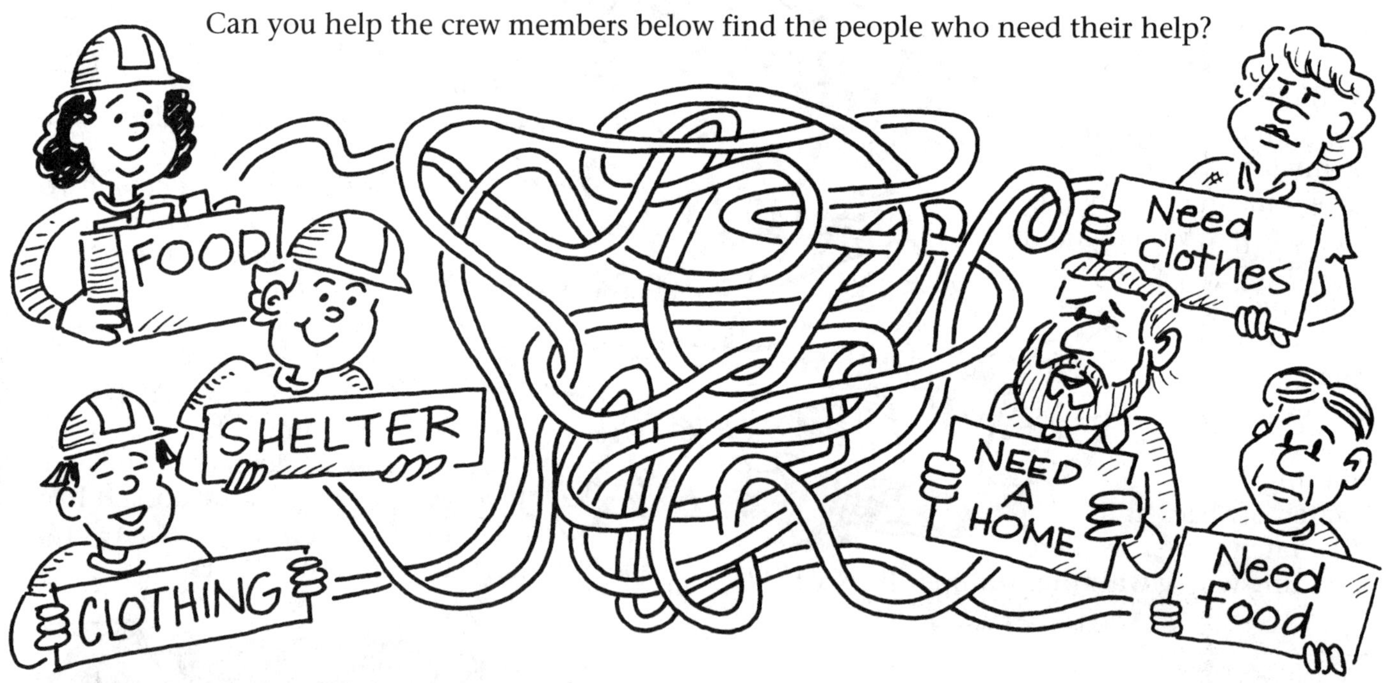

CREW SKILL PRACTICE

- Use the Power Source Prayer today.
- Add a compliment to your list.
- Ask a parent or teacher to tell you how your church cares for the needy in your town. See if you can help.
- Work on Bible Blueprint Verse 6 (page 10). Did you recognize it in today's Bible reading?
- Look for a chance to tell someone about Jesus today. Or invite that person to church or church club.
- Record your work points.

CHECK THE MASTER PLAN: Read James 2:14–17

THINK ABOUT IT: "Actions speak louder than words!" Have you heard this wise saying before? It sort of sums up the verses you just read in James, doesn't it? True faith in Jesus should change us. It should show in the way we treat other people. Would handing a booklet or tract about Jesus to a hungry, homeless person be the best way to help him or her?

____

Why? (If you answered no, explain what you would do instead.)

____

When telling others about Jesus, we should choose our words carefully. Some of the best words we can choose are words we put into action rather than just talk about. Here are 10 words God would like to see all of his crew members put into action. Can you find them in the word search puzzle? Put a star by the ones you've put into action during the Adventure.

FORGIVE SHARE LOVE CHEER
HELP LISTEN WELCOME
BEFRIEND SUPPORT TEACH

```
K R F E L L O T E A C H T S
R S U P P O R T T S O A E W
O T B E F U N E F A R M P E
A F R A D I D N O I E E W L
P P O R N T S U R L G E E S
H C H E E R T C G A L T L R
S H E E I R F O I C O B C E
H L L V R E L O V E V P O F
A L P O F O L L E W P I M R
R G I N E O T E L I S T E N
E Y O U B R A C H U E N D H
F O R G E S T G S L P E S H
```

- Plug into the Power Source Prayer.
- Add a compliment to your list and share one with a friend.
- Work on Bible Blueprint Verse 6 (page 10).
- Talk to someone about Jesus today. Or invite that person to church or church club.
- Record your work points.

ANSWERS:

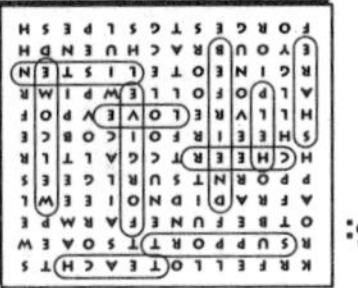

SATURDAY, DAY 42

LEVEL CHECK

WEEK 7 (5 POINTS)

The end of the Adventure is drawing near. Have you learned anything new about being an active member of God's crew? We hope so, because kids like you are an important part of God's family. You'll take the message about Jesus into the future. Someday you'll be the grown-ups who will teach a whole new generation of kids about how to belong to God's forever family.

BIBLE BLUEPRINT

VERSE CHECK

VERSE 7 (10 POINTS)

Turn to page 10 to find this week's Bible Blueprint Verse. It tells us two things we can do when we meet with the Master Builder, Jesus. Try one of the following ideas to help you memorize it.

1. Say it like a cheer!

It is good. It is good. It is good to praise.
It is good to praise the Lord. (clap, clap)
To sing, to sing, praises to God,
Praises to God Most High. (clap, clap)
Psalm, Psalm
Psalm 92,
Psalm 92, verse 1 (clap, clap)

2. Sing it to the tune of "Michael Rowed the Boat Ashore."

It is good to praise the Lord, Alleluia!
It is good to praise the Lord, Alleluia!
To sing praise to God Most High, Alleluia!
To sing praise to God Most High, Alleluia!

CREW SKILL PRACTICE

- Choose a new person to pray for in your Power Source Prayers this week.
- Add a church compliment to your list. Do you have 42 yet?
- Work on learning Bible Blueprint Verse 7 (page 10) and record your work points.

SUNDAY, DAY 43

CHECK THE MASTER PLAN:
Read Acts 4:23–31

THINK ABOUT IT: For many years a crippled man sat by the temple gates. He begged his living from the crowds coming to worship. When Peter used God's power to heal him in Jesus' name, the news quickly spread all over the city. The religious leaders of the temple were angry. They tried to threaten Peter and John to keep them from preaching. Their threats worried the believers, but that didn't stop them. They turned to God for help and courage. They knew who was really in charge of the world. It wasn't the high priest. It wasn't King Herod. It wasn't Pontius Pilate.

It was __ __ __. It still is __ __ __. And it always will be __ __ __. What do you need God to help you with today? Pray about it when you meet with the Master Builder, Jesus.

CREW SKILL PRACTICE

- If you didn't do it yesterday, choose a new person to pray for this week.
- Add a church compliment to your list. Do you have 43 yet?
- Work on learning Bible Blueprint Verse 7 (page 10) and record your work points.

ANSWERS: 1-P, 2-PM, 3-P, 4-PM/KQ, 5-P, 6-PM, 7-PM, 8-K/Q

Do you know which countries are led by a president (P), a prime minister (PM), or a king/queen (K/Q)? Circle the answers you believe are correct.

1. UNITED STATES	P	PM	K/Q
2. CANADA	P	PM	K/Q
3. MEXICO	P	PM	K/Q
4. ENGLAND	P	PM	K/Q
5. SOUTH AFRICA	P	PM	K/Q
6. JAPAN	P	PM	K/Q
7. ISRAEL	P	PM	K/Q
8. SAUDI ARABIA	P	PM	K/Q

Remember, even though these people are the leaders of their countries, God is the real leader. He is the Master Builder of the world. Isn't it something that we can meet with him every day?

Earn 2 bonus points each for naming the government leaders above. (It's OK to look up the names or ask for help.)

MONDAY, DAY 44

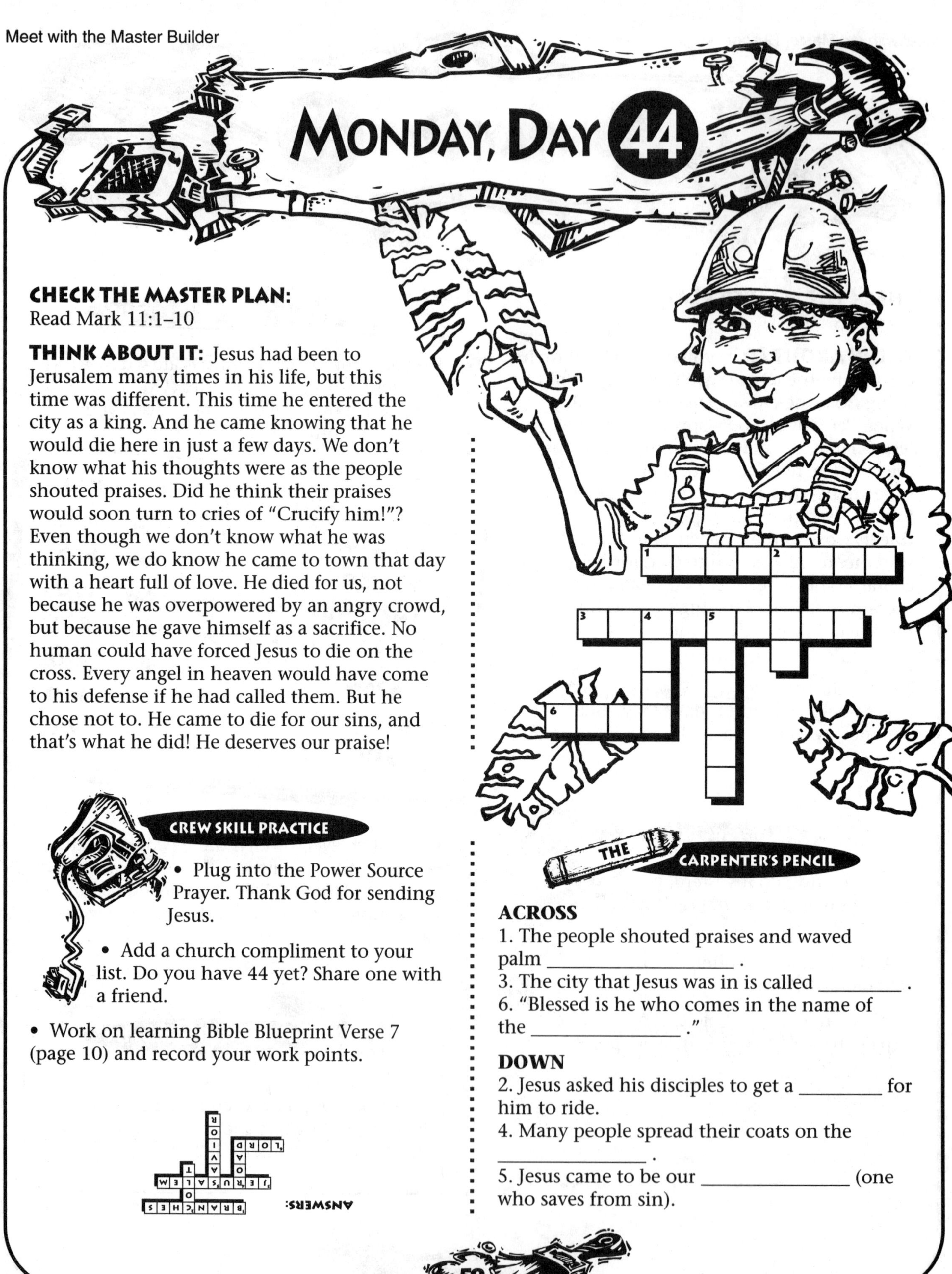

CHECK THE MASTER PLAN:
Read Mark 11:1–10

THINK ABOUT IT: Jesus had been to Jerusalem many times in his life, but this time was different. This time he entered the city as a king. And he came knowing that he would die here in just a few days. We don't know what his thoughts were as the people shouted praises. Did he think their praises would soon turn to cries of "Crucify him!"? Even though we don't know what he was thinking, we do know he came to town that day with a heart full of love. He died for us, not because he was overpowered by an angry crowd, but because he gave himself as a sacrifice. No human could have forced Jesus to die on the cross. Every angel in heaven would have come to his defense if he had called them. But he chose not to. He came to die for our sins, and that's what he did! He deserves our praise!

CREW SKILL PRACTICE

- Plug into the Power Source Prayer. Thank God for sending Jesus.
- Add a church compliment to your list. Do you have 44 yet? Share one with a friend.
- Work on learning Bible Blueprint Verse 7 (page 10) and record your work points.

THE CARPENTER'S PENCIL

ACROSS
1. The people shouted praises and waved palm ________________ .
3. The city that Jesus was in is called ________ .
6. "Blessed is he who comes in the name of the ______________ ."

DOWN
2. Jesus asked his disciples to get a ________ for him to ride.
4. Many people spread their coats on the ______________ .
5. Jesus came to be our ______________ (one who saves from sin).

ANSWERS: 1. BRANCHES 2. COLT 3. JERUSALEM 4. ROAD 5. SAVIOR 6. LORD

TUESDAY, DAY 45

CHECK THE MASTER PLAN:
Read Psalm 84:1–4, 10–12

THINK ABOUT IT: If you could go anywhere you wanted to, where would it be? Would it be church? Most kids your age would probably choose to go someplace they thought was more fun. But the writer of this psalm had learned something: being close to God can bring you joy. Praising God can bring joy not only to you, but to others as well. If your parents or friends love Jesus, they probably feel joy when they see and hear you praise God. Does it make you feel joyful inside when you go to church and sing his praises?

THE CARPENTER'S PENCIL

How many times is the word "JOYFUL" written on the swallow's nest? First take a guess; then count. (Words can wrap from the end of one line to the start of the next.)

JOYFULJOYFULJOYFULJOYFULJOYFULJOYFULJO
YFULJOYFULJOYFULJOYFULJOYFULJOYFULJOYF
ULJOYFULJOYFULJOYFULJOYFULJOYFULJOYFUL
JOYFULJOYFULJOYFULJOYFULJOYFULJOYFULJO
YFULJOYFULJOYFULJOYFULJOYFULJOYFULJOYF
ULJOYFULJOYFULJOYFULJOYFULJOYFULJOYFUL
JOYFULJOYFULJOYFULJOYFULJOYFULJOYFULJO
YFULJOYFULJOYFULJOYFULJOYFULJOYFULJOYF
ULJOYFULJOYFULJOYFULJOYFULJOYFULJOYFUL
JOYFULJOYFULJOYFULJOYFULJOYFULJOYFULJO
YFULJOYFULJOYFULJOYFULJOYFULJOYFUL

MY GUESS ______ **MY COUNT** ______

CREW SKILL PRACTICE

- Don't forget to power up with prayer. Sing God a praise song. Do you know one with the word "joy" or "joyful" in it?
- Add another compliment to your list. (See pages 33–34.)
- Review Bible Blueprint Verse 7 (page 10) and record your work points.

ANSWERS: 69 TIMES

WEDNESDAY, DAY 46

CHECK THE MASTER PLAN:
Read 1 Timothy 3:14–16

THINK ABOUT IT: These verses are part of Paul's first letter to his friend Timothy. Timothy was preaching and teaching at the church Paul had started in the town of Ephesus. To what kind of God does Paul say the church belongs?

The **(GILNIV)** __ __ __ __ __ __ God. (Unscramble the word.)

Then, Paul reminds Timothy of some other wonderful truths about God. Here are some truths you need to remember:

1. When Jesus was born, God came in human form to live with people.

2. At Jesus' baptism, God's Holy Spirit spoke from heaven and said, "You are my Son, whom I love; with you I am well pleased."

3. When Satan tried to tempt Jesus to sin, Jesus refused. God's angels helped Jesus.

4. The good news about Jesus spread from town to town and from nation to nation.

5. Jesus is in heaven now preparing a place for his followers. He is not dead. He is alive and getting ready to come back to earth again someday.

Has anyone ever told you these things about God? If you have any questions about Jesus, ask someone at home or church to help you answer them.

OVERTIME OPPORTUNITY

(15 Bonus Points)

Do you like to jump rope? Try making up a jumping rhyme that tells about some of the things our living God can do.

THE CARPENTER'S PENCIL

What are some of the wonderful things our living God can do? Write about three things. It's OK to ask someone for ideas.

1. **GOD CAN** ______________________________
____
____

2. **GOD CAN** ______________________________
____
____

3. **GOD CAN** ______________________________
____
____

CREW SKILL PRACTICE

- Don't forget to power up with prayer. Praise God for the wonderful things he can do.
- Add another compliment to your list.
- Review Bible Blueprint Verse 7 (page 10) and record your work points.

Second On-the-Job Training Topic for Week 7:
Celebrate the best
club ever

Thursday, Day 47

CHECK THE MASTER PLAN:
Read Matthew 16:13–21

THINK ABOUT IT: Have you ever peeked at the end of a story you were reading to find how it was going to end? Well, you're not alone if you have. Waiting to find out what's going to happen next can be really hard sometimes. Jesus knew that, and that's why he told his disciples the things you just read about in Matthew. He wanted them to be prepared. In verse 21, what four things did he say would happen?

1. He would go to the city of _______________ .

2. He would ____________________ a lot.

3. He would be ____________________________ .

4. And after three days, he would ____________

____ .

Did all four things come true? (Get help if you need it for this one.)

____

____

CREW SKILL PRACTICE

- Continue praying for the person you chose last weekend.
- Add another compliment to your list.
- Record your work points.

BIBLE BLUEPRINT

VERSE CHECK

VERSE 8 (10 POINTS)

This last verse, 1 Peter 2:9, is about celebrating being a part of God's family. (You'll find it on page 10.) To help you memorize this Bible Blueprint Verse, try making a Mobius word strip. To make one follow these directions:

1. Cut a strip of paper 2 feet long. (Tape shorter pieces together if you have to.)

2. Bring the ends of the strip together to make a loop. Then turn one of the ends upside down, and tape the ends together.

3. Write the verse in pencil on the strip. If you have room, write it more than once.

4. To practice, read the verse over and over again. When you think you're starting to learn it, erase some of the words and keep saying the verse.

FRIDAY, DAY 48

CHECK THE MASTER PLAN:
Read Psalm 22:9–18, 24–31

THINK ABOUT IT: Almost 1000 years before Jesus was born, the Spirit of God helped King David write the words to this psalm. What parts of verses 9–18 remind you of Jesus' death on the cross? If you need help, look at Mark 15:21–30, 33–37.

____

____

____

What good things do verses 25–31 tell us we can look forward to someday?

____

____

____

The end of our Adventure is a good time to celebrate being a part of God's family. It's like being a member of the best club ever! Everyone can join. Everyone is welcome.

CREW SKILL PRACTICE

- Use the Power Source Prayer.
- Add another compliment to your list. Share one with a friend.
- Have you invited someone to church yet? This weekend would be a good time.
- Review Bible Blueprint Verse 8 (page 10) and record your work points.

THE CARPENTER'S PENCIL

Create a picture by copying the lines in each box below into the boxes on the grid at the bottom of the page. Match the numbers and letters. What does this picture have to do with your Bible reading for today?

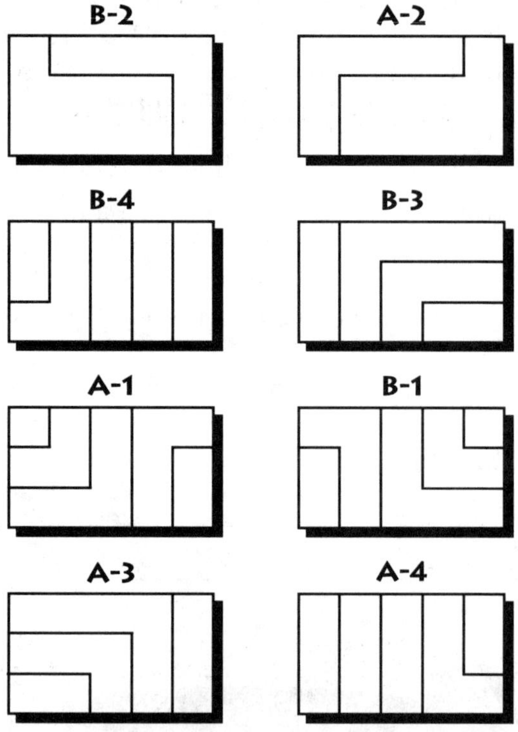

B-2 A-2

B-4 B-3

A-1 B-1

A-3 A-4

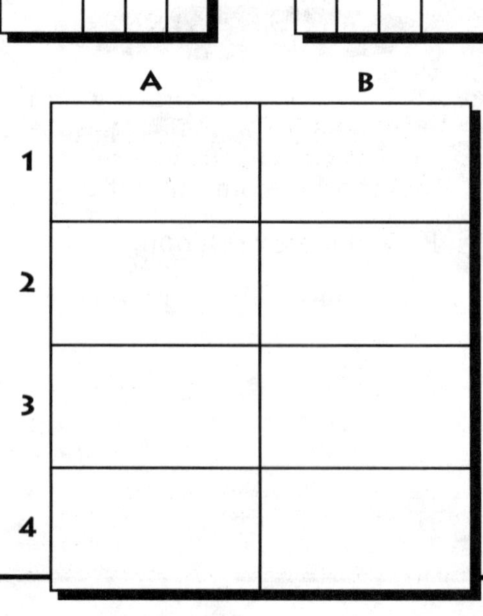

SATURDAY, DAY 49

CHECK THE MASTER PLAN: Read 1 Peter 1:3–9

THINK ABOUT IT: Have you ever gotten a splinter in your skin? It hurts, doesn't it? And getting it out can hurt even more. But if you trust someone to help you, once it's gone, the healing begins. Doubts and fears are like splinters in our heart. God wants us to trust him to help us get rid of these painful feelings and worries. He uses the difficult times in our lives to help us learn that we can have faith in him. What he has promised us, he will do. And one of the most important things he has promised to do, is to forgive our sins and give us everlasting life. Now that's something to celebrate this weekend with the other members of God's crew.

Being a part of God's crew is like being a part of a great club. Decode the words to the club cheer below by adding one straight line to each letter.

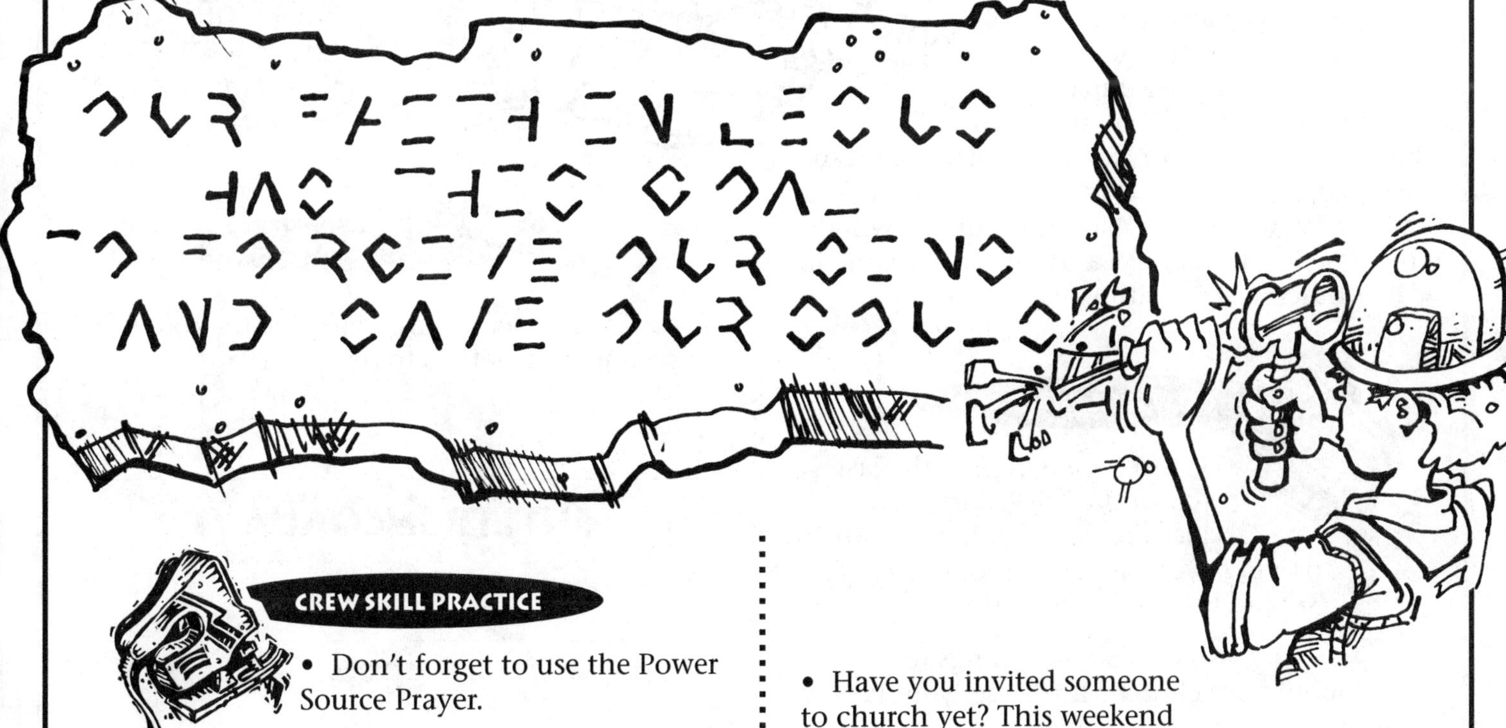

CREW SKILL PRACTICE

- Don't forget to use the Power Source Prayer.
- Go over Bible Blueprint Verse 8 (page 10).
- Add another compliment to your list. Do you have 49 things on your list yet?
- Have you invited someone to church yet? This weekend would be a good time.
- Record your work points. It's OK to go back and do some activities you missed if you want to earn some more points.

ANSWER: OUR FAITH IN JESUS HAS THIS GOAL: TO FORGIVE OUR SINS AND SAVE OUR SOULS.

SUNDAY, DAY 50

CHECK THE MASTER PLAN:
Read Acts 9:1–19

THINK ABOUT IT: Getting to know Jesus can be a life-changing event. The apostle Paul you read about many days during the Adventure was a faithful man. He willingly faced great dangers to tell others about Jesus. But Paul wasn't always that kind of man. The story you just read about a man named Saul is the story of how Paul became a Christian. (Yes, he changed his name.) Before he met Jesus, he was a Christian's worst nightmare, or at least one of the worst. He hunted Christians down and had them arrested and sometimes killed. Not a nice man! But Jesus changed all that. Isn't it great to know that God can forgive and save a man like Saul? He will do the same for us, too. Ask a parent or someone in your church to talk with you about that.

CREW SKILL PRACTICE

- Just because this is the last day of the Adventure, that doesn't mean you have to stop praying every day. This is one habit you should keep for a lifetime.
- Did you find 50 nice things to say about your church? If not, get your family or some church friends to help you.
- Did you learn Bible Blueprint Verse 8 (page 10)?
- Record your work points and remember to congratulate yourself for your skill! What did you learn on this Adventure?

THE CARPENTER'S PENCIL

The Adventure crew has a message for you. Just unscramble the letters to decode it.

____

SNTLTRGNCOAUAIO

______ **DAN**   ______ **EEPK**   ______ **PU**

______ **HTE**   ______ **DGOO**   ______ **KROW**!

ANSWER: CONGRATULATIONS AND KEEP UP THE GOOD WORK!